FLYER LIVES

FLYER LIVES

Philadelphia Hockey Greats
Share Their Personal Stories

JAKKI CLARKE

TRIUMPH
B O O K S

Library of Congress Cataloging-in-Publication Data

Clarke, Jakki Lyn.
  Flyer lives : Philadelphia hockey greats share their personal stories / by Jakki Lyn Clarke.
    p. cm.
  ISBN 978-1-60078-756-0
  1. Philadelphia Flyers (Hockey team) 2. Hockey players—Anecdotes.
I. Title.
  GV848.P48C53 2012
  796.962'640974811—dc23

2012017091

This book is available in quantity at special discounts for your group or organization. For further information, contact:

Triumph Books
  814 North Franklin Street
  Chicago, Illinois 60610
  (312) 337-0747
  www.triumphbooks.com

Printed in U.S.A.

ISBN: 978-1-60078-756-0

Cover design by Andy Hansen

Interior design by Amy Carter

Photos courtesy of AP Images: pages xi, 14, 221, 232, and 246; Getty Images: 28, 42, 52, 56, 68, 82, 92, 102, 116, 128, 138, 158, 170, 182, 194, 206, and 256; and 271 courtesy of the author.

This book is dedicated to

the best sports fans

of any city in the world...

your passion is unmatched, and

your support is cherished.

When God made Philly fans,

He broke the mold.

Thank you all.

"Ya know, they always say if you live in one place long enough, you are that place."

—Rocky Balboa

CONTENTS

FOREWORD

I'll never forget the first time I saw a hockey game. I immediately fell in love with the sport and I knew right away that a team could work in Philadelphia. I was fortunate that the National Hockey League was expanding and I was able to create the Philadelphia Flyers.

Our first several years were tough, but through Keith Allen's tremendous drafting and his ability to put together an amazing roster, and Fred Shero's outstanding leadership on the bench, we won the Stanley Cup in 1974 and again in 1975. The Flyers have and continued to be one of the toughest teams in the National Hockey League, and I'm very proud of that.

I have always looked at the players who played for the Flyers as my family. Reading some of these terrific chapters has been a wonderful journey down memory lane.

This book is a sampling of the fine athletes we've been lucky enough to watch perform, night after night, despite injury, despite daunting odds...that have kept us on the edge of our seats and dazzled us; that have known the thrill of triumph, as well as the agony of defeat, and have allowed us along for the amazing ride.

Winning, of course, is always the ultimate goal. But something that often goes overlooked is the unbreakable bond between teammates. The willingness to sacrifice oneself and not think of it as sacrifice at all, the friendships, the solidarity, the determination to pick each other up no matter how tired, how black and blue. This indestructible brotherhood is found few other places besides a locker room.

The unmovable commitment and loyalty I have witnessed over the years—to one another, to the Flyers family, and to our fans, the most loyal fans in any sport—has astounded me at times, and is perhaps what I am most proud of: the Brotherhood of the Orange and Black.

And I hope each of you will love reading their stories as much as I did…

Let's Go Flyers!

—Ed Snider

CHAPTER 1

BERNIE PARENT

If you happen to be at the Wells Fargo Center during any given home game, it isn't uncommon to see the Flyers Ambassador of Hockey strolling the concourse; laughing, joking, and shaking hands with his fans; signing autographs happily; and telling stories in that unmistakable voice still draped in a lovely French accent, his retired No. 1 jersey hanging from the rafters in the backdrop.

Or maybe you watched the 2012 Winter Classic Alumni Game where before a crowd of 45,000 at Citizen's Bank Park, he—at age 66—started in goal for the Flyers; played for five minutes, letting in no goals on five shots, and earning him the First Star of the game to a raucous standing ovation.

Like most Canadian boys, Bernie Parent learned to skate on the frozen ponds of his hometown. A true original in every way, however, even Bernie's hockey beginnings were unique.

———

The year is 1956.

Boxer Rocky Marciano retires as the only undefeated heavyweight champion of the world with a perfect record (49–0) while the Philadelphia Warriors win 4–1 against the Fort Wayne Pistons to become NBA champions.

The talk of the baseball world is the Subway Series, which saw Jackie Robinson's last major league hit. The New York Yankees—the Bronx Bombers—clinch the title in seven games against the Brooklyn Dodgers at the last World Series game ever to be played at Brooklyn's Ebbets Field, with legendary pitching by Yankee Don Larsen, who throws the only perfect game in World Series history during Game 5 and earns MVP honors.[1]

And Bernie Parent, age 11, is first learning to skate.

Why such a late start?

"I was the youngest of seven kids, and my dad was just an average working man that didn't make much money. So we only had one pair of skates. I had to wait my turn," he says.

"I was a late bloomer. I started later than the usual kid, and I wanted to be a defenseman. So I put the skates on—by the way, they were too big," he says. "So I put them on, put on the equipment, and you had to go around the ice once, and depending on your speed, the coach could figure out where you should

---

1. This marked the only no-hitter thrown in any postseason game until October 6, 2010, when—in his first postseason appearance—Philadelphia Phillie Roy Halladay pitched a no-hitter against the Cincinnati Reds in the National League Divisonal Series.

play. So the first kid goes around in 14 seconds, 15 maybe. So my turn came, and I did mine in 22 seconds. And the coach looked at me and pointed and said, 'Goaltender!'

"I said, 'Sure, why not?' I had played goal in the streets in Montreal. You have to remember, the streets in Montreal in those days—it was a long time ago—they left the ice on the streets for the whole winter because they didn't have chemicals then [to melt the ice]. They only had sand. So I always played goal with boots on. I had never played goal with skates on. So the first game I played goal on skates with all of the equipment on and the whole bit, they scored 21 goals against me. And the coach said, 'Get the hell outta here!' I wasn't that smart, but I was smart enough to realize that I should start playing in the street with the skates on, which I started doing. And two weeks later, somehow his goalie got hurt, and Coach called me out of desperation. He didn't have anybody else. And I said, 'I've been practicing with skates on!', and we won that game 5–3. Then I was on my way."

———

Parent's childhood hero was Montreal Canadiens goaltender Jacques Plante, whose sister lived next door to Parent.

"My passion as a little kid was to win the Stanley Cup. And of course every Saturday night was *Hockey Night in Canada*. I used to watch him and just say, 'Wow.' And then once a summer—I'll never forget this—he would come over to visit his sister, and I'd be watching. I knew when he was coming, and I'd be watching from the window. I didn't want to meet him because I was too scared," he says. "And then I'd see him getting out of the car, smoking his cigar, and what a great feeling that was, getting to see him. And to this day, I smoke cigars, too."

Plante would go on to play a significant role in Parent's career later in life as well, but we're getting a bit ahead of ourselves.

Bernie Parent began his career in the Boston Bruins' minor league system in 1963.

Parent says: "So there I am, 17 years old [with] the Boston Bruins in the National Hockey League…'Wow!' You know what I'm saying? 'This is cool!' And we celebrated the whole summer…and then it was the first time in my life I dealt with taking risk and dealing with fear. Because September came and reality set in. I had to get on the train and go to Niagara Falls [the farm team of the Bruins at that time], and I had to leave the safety of my family, my house, my friends. I got on the train with my suitcase by myself and had to go to Niagara Falls, and I couldn't speak English. So all the glory and excitement I had during the summer went out the window. Reality hit pretty hard."

Parent appeared in 39 games with the Bruins and spent the following season splitting his time between the Bruins and their farm club in Oklahoma. Left unprotected for the 1967 NHL Expansion Draft, Parent was picked up by the Flyers, where he went on to record a 2.48 GAA with four shutouts, helping the Flyers finish first in the West Division. Although initially he split his time in the net with fellow goaltender Doug Favell, over the next two seasons, Favell—another former Bruin prospect—had difficulty with injuries and inconsistent play, pushing Parent to the slot of Flyers No. 1 goalie.

While Parent's English-speaking skills were a never-ending source of amusement for his teammates—particularly when he was excited—there was a serious side to it, too. During the early days of his career, he did not conduct interviews in English for fear of saying the wrong things.

But ever the optimist, Parent seems to find the silver lining in every situation.

"I had chemistry with the other players. Human beings are generally pretty good. They know when you're struggling with something, and they try to help you out. But there's a good side to not understanding what people are saying," he says. "Because when criticism came, I didn't understand what they were saying. So that was cool. It worked both ways."

Then disaster struck.

It's the winter of 1971. It's the debut of a new stock market index called the Nasdaq, as well as the landmark television sitcom *All In The Family*, starring Carroll O'Connor as Archie Bunker. Backed by American air and artillery support, South Vietnamese troops invade Laos, and Evel Knievel sets a world record and jumps 19 cars in Ontario, California.

As part of a strategy to improve the team's offense, the Flyers traded Parent to the Maple Leafs, a move that turned out to be a great windfall of luck for the Flyers[2], but not so much for Bernie, at least not at first.

"When I got traded from the Flyers to Toronto, it was a very low point in my career," he says. "But little did I know I was going to get to spend two years with Jacques [Plante] in Toronto. And that changed my whole career. Sometimes you have to hit bottom to realize where you want to be."

At the time Plante, age 42, was having an All-Star season, and under his tutelage Parent improved his skills as a technically proficient goalie, leading to more consistent play. Throughout the 1971–72 season, Parent played well for the Leafs, but—perhaps most important—he gained valuable regular season and playoff experience.

"When I got on the team with him, I'd just watch him and say 'Wow.' Yes, I had God-given talent—I mean to play in the National Hockey League you have to have God-given talent—but

---

2. The Flyers received Mike Walton and a first-round draft pick from Toronto along with goalie Bruce Gamble. Immediately they flipped Walton to the Bruins for Rick MacLeish and Danny Schock.

This trade is remarkable because MacLeish became a Flyers legend, scoring 328 goals in the Orange and Black in addition to 54 in the playoffs. Perhaps most notably, however, was MacLeish's Cup-clinching goal in Game 6 of the 1974 Stanley Cup Finals against the Bruins to give the Flyers their first championship. A consistent 30-goal scorer in the regular season, MacLeish had a way of shining in the playoffs: he led the NHL in playoff scoring during the Flyers' runs to the Cups in '74 and '75.

I didn't have the understanding of the game," he says. "And what I got from those two years with him was I got to understand the game. What I mean by this is how to study the defensemen, how they play—a left-hand shot versus a right-hand shot, what to do in different situations like two-on-ones, stuff like this. And the communication between defensemen and a goalie is very, very important because they also have to know what you [the goaltender] are doing, how you'll react in this situation or that. So when you work as a team like this, you have a much better chance of making the save. And I didn't have that before. So when I spent the two years [with Plante], then I got the understanding of the game, and that changed my whole career."

But, of course, Parent eventually returned to Philly.

After the Maple Leafs left him without a contract the following summer, Parent signed a large contract with the Miami Screaming Eagles of the newly formed World Hockey Association, becoming the first NHL player to do so. But the Eagles did not emerge as planned and instead became the Philadelphia Blazers. After a contract dispute prompted him to leave the team, Parent wanted to return to the NHL but did not wish to return to the Leafs. Toronto traded Parent's NHL rights back to the Flyers for Favell, his former teammate, and a first round pick in that summer's amateur draft.

"When I came back to the Flyers, I was ready," Parent says. "And the team was ready. And we had a really good combination."

The next two seasons were the greatest of his career. Playing 73 games of a 78-game schedule, Parent led the league with a 1.89 GAA and 12 shutouts, shared the Vezina Trophy[3] with Chicago's Tony Esposito[4], was named a first team All-Star, and helped lead the Flyers to a first-place finish in the West Division. He went on to win the Conn Smythe Trophy (playoff MVP) as the Flyers won their first of consecutive Stanley Cup championships. The following year he won another Vezina Trophy, a second Conn Smythe Trophy, and another Stanley Cup, creating the popular catchphrase: "Only the Lord saves more than Bernie Parent," a sentiment that appeared on countless bumper stickers.

"There were so many good teams," he says. "But you know what we had? We had charisma. When you look at the Flyers, I think we bonded with the city. Although we were hated everywhere else, we bonded with the city and it was one big family, and it's been that way ever since and is still that way today. And that's something to cherish forever.

"Let me give you a good example: in 1967, when we got introduced to the city, they put us on the float and we went through the city on Broad Street, and about 10 people showed

---

3. Named in honor of Georges Vezina—a standout goaltender of the Montreal Canadiens from 1910 until 1925 who died in 1926 of tuberculosis.

4. A standout goalie for the Blackhawks, Tony Esposito (the younger brother of Phil Esposito) a center who had a notable career and also is enshrined in the Hockey Hall of Fame), was not only one of the pioneers of the now popular butterfly style but also is one of just eight goalies to win the Vezina catching the puck right-handed.

up," he says. "Seven years later, we won the Stanley Cup and we had over 2 million people. I've always said this and I will always say it, 75 percent of our success was from the people of the Delaware Valley. The support that we received from the people was incredible.

"As an athlete you have to learn that when you're playing well and you get the praise, it's great, but when you're not playing well, you also have to be able to accept criticism. It's very, very important. So you prepare yourself to step on the ice, and the expectation [of the fans] brings you to a different level that makes you perform better."

Following the championship seasons, Parent was sidelined by injury, appearing in only 11 games in 1975–76, and experienced difficulties during the next three seasons. Although retired at the time, Parent's childhood hero continued to have a strong influence on Parent's career, and, at one point when Parent was playing poorly and considering retirement, Plante flew to Philly to help. Both were stand-up-type goalies, and as Plante watched Parent practice, he diagnosed the problem: Parent was sitting back on his heels, backing into his crease and losing concentration. He heeded Plante's advice and transformed his play once again at the top of his game.

It, however, was to be short-lived. In February 1979 Parent suffered a career-ending eye injury in a game against the New York Rangers when an errant stick entered the right eyehole of his mask, causing permanent damage to his vision. This incident triggered many NHL goalies to switch from fiberglass facemasks to the cage-and-helmet style and resulted in many amateur and junior leagues mandating the helmet/cage combo, banning fiberglass masks altogether.

But Bernie's memories of his time on the ice remain positive and fond as well as his time off the ice—when he and his teammates would play pranks on one another.

Bernie remembers one of his favorites: "Ross Lonsberry[5] used to wear a wig all the time, and one day I got out of practice early and I took scissors and cut the wig in half. But the problem was, he suffered a leg injury and he came out of practice early…right after I did. So he walked in and he caught me with the wig and the scissors in my hand," he says. "And to this day, I always deny it. I say, 'I just happened to be there and picked it up. It was somebody else.' So it's funny now, but it wasn't at the time."

The best advice Parent ever received from a coach came from the notable Fred Shero. "Freddy had glasses, and he'd always push them back with his finger. And when I came back with the Flyers, he looked at me in the eyes—this was the first time I ever met him—and he said, 'I don't know anything about

---

5. A left winger who played 15 NHL seasons with the Bruins, Kings, and Penguins, Ross Lonsberry's best seasons were spent as a Broad Street Bully, winning the Cup twice. Lonsberry played in 100 career playoff matches, scoring 21 goals and 25 assists, and finished his career with 566 points (256 goals and 310 assists) and 806 penalty minutes in 968 games.

goaltending; you're on your own,' and I said, 'Bingo!' I loved it. What he meant by this was: you play as a team, but as an individual you do your own stuff. So you have a system as a team, but as an individual you have the freedom to do the things you want to do. And that to me was awesome."

Does the Hockey Hall of Famer—ranked No. 63 on *The Hockey News*' list of the 100 Greatest Hockey Players—who mentored future Vezina-winning goalies Ron Hextall and the late Pelle Lindbergh have any advice of his own to give?

"The advice I would give to parents is to ask your kids a very, very important question that nobody asks kids anymore and probably never did," he says. "And the question is: 'What's your passion? What would you love to do for the rest of your life?' And let the kid think about it for weeks, maybe months, and let them know that everybody has a passion. And then I would ask the kids as they're going toward their passion, 'Who do you surround yourself with? And the people you're surrounding yourself with, are they going in circles, or do they have great ideas and want to go someplace in life?' So those would be the two questions I'd ask as a parent, and then support [the kids]. You may not agree with what they want to do, but that's their life. It's not yours.

"A career is part of your journey in life. So there's before, career, and after. You go through different phases. Now if you look at my 'career,' I'm proud of the Stanley Cup, of course, but it's also [being able] to overcome obstacles and having a 'never quit' attitude. It's so easy to quit in life, and I always said, 'Why assume it's not going to work out?' I always said, 'Try. And if you don't like it, learn from it and move on.' So having a 'never quit attitude' is very, very important.

"My motivation was my passion. And you know, you could describe passion as your purpose. I think back to when I took my suitcase and went to Niagara Falls to take the train to Boston. I always ask myself the question: 'Why did I go?' And today I've finally got the answer. The only reason that kept me going was the passion to win the Stanley Cup. If I didn't have the passion, I would've chosen something else. I would've backed off and done something else. So purpose and passion is very, very important to whatever you're doing in life. That's the motivation that keeps you going through the ups and downs through your career and through your life. If you have a purpose and the passion, you have the motivation to keep moving forward. I was talking to a group of students—seniors—just before the last day of school in June. And I asked them, 'What is your purpose?' And none of them could answer me. Then one kid raised his hand and said, 'How do you define 'purpose?' It was a good question. And I said, 'I'll tell you how to define purpose…find out what you love to do, what your passion is—not for your parents or your friends, your sister or brother, or whatever—for *you*. You're a unique person. Look at your fingerprints. Nobody's like you in this world. Find out what you love to do, what you dream about…and that becomes your purpose—and go for it.'"

And nobody is quite like you either, Bernie.

CHAPTER 2

BOBBY CLARKE

Settled in 1915 by prospectors in search of gold, the city of Flin
Flon is nestled in the heart of Northern Manitoba's picturesque
lake country. This small, close-knit community is known for
things such as Manitoba's largest copper mine and—aside from
Tarzana, California—is the only North American city to be
named after a fictional character in a novel.

What is perhaps most astonishing, however, is that this
isolated hamlet also nurtured several NHL players, including Gerry Hart, who played 730 NHL games, as well as Ted
Hampson (who was the second player ever to receive the Bill
Masterton Trophy[6]). It has turned out numerous NHLers who
played junior hockey there, prompting many a baffled observer
to marvel, "There must be something in the water."

Although those prospectors may not have found the glitter-
ing mineral they so doggedly sought after, those who followed

---

6. Selected by the *Professional Hockey Writers' Association* after each team
nominates one player, the Bill Masterton Memorial Trophy is awarded annually
to the NHL player who best exemplifies the qualities of perseverance, sportsman-
ship, and dedication to the game. It is often awarded to a player who has come
back from career-threatening or even life-threatening illness or injury.

them most certainly found hockey gold amid "The City Built on Rocks."

About 2,200 miles from Philadelphia, it shares the same latitude as Moscow, is covered in snow roughly nine months of the year, and boasts an average high of 3 degrees Fahrenheit in January.

It is also the home of Bobby Clarke.

Born in 1949, the same year the Eagles drafted Chuck "Concrete Charlie" Bednarik (first pick overall), Clarke remembers his early years: "The township had an outdoor rink at the corner of our road, and all the kids played hockey. The fathers cleaned the snow off [the pond]. We were all pretty young at the start. I was only three or four, but, of course, as we got older we cleaned it ourselves. You'd put your skates on in the basement [of your house], and then off you went. You skated down the street, and you went to the rink and played hockey.

"We never played indoors until we were eight or nine when we were put on teams by the township. We played against each other in the arena on Saturday mornings—a game a week for 15 weeks—until you were 12 and you were able to move up and play at night. And maybe at that time you played probably 20 games a year, maybe 25. That was indoors. But, of course, we only played those few games indoors; everything else was all outdoors.

"For whatever reason, I just loved playing hockey. I can't honestly tell you why I loved it so much. And lots of other kids in Flin Flon did, too, just as much as me. But when we were about 12 or 13, we got television. So that was kind of the dividing line between those who played but didn't like it as much and those of us who did…the rest of us? We played all the time. Any chance we could get on the ice, we did. Whether it was outdoors or indoors, or some people had rinks in their backyards… it didn't matter. We just wanted to play."

———

The year is 1965, and 3,500 U.S. Marines have just arrived in Saigon, becoming the first American combat troops in Vietnam, essentially beginning the war, while The Beatles set a new world record for crowd attendance (more than 55,600) when they play at New York's Shea Stadium, becoming the first musicians to play at such a large venue.

And Bobby Clarke, age 16, has been pumping gas at the town's only service station and saving up all summer so he can buy a new pair of skates.

"Pretty much in those days, you just played in skates that had been used before. Sometimes you got a new pair, but not very often," he says. "You just kind of passed them around."

But Bobby was gearing up to go to his first junior camp and had his heart set on a new pair. So he tracked down a shoemaker who also made skates in Brandon, Manitoba.

"I had saved $100, and the skates cost 60, which was really, *really* expensive for skates in those days," he says.

And so young Bobby set out on a mission.

Alongside him was Flin Flon Bombers stick boy Bill McIntyre[7], then nine years old, and off they went hitchhiking 875 round-trip miles so Bobby could get fitted for his new skates.[8]

"I think we were gone for about four days," he recalls vaguely as if it were a trip down around the block.

When asked if his parents knew where he was at the time, he laughed. "No, no. Actually I never would've gone if they'd known. It was the end of the summer, and they were on vacation for a week, and I was old enough to stay by myself. My little sister had gone with them. So I was home alone, and I figured it was as good of a time to go as any," he says with a mischievous grin. "I wouldn't have gone if they were home. They never would've let me, even though hitchhiking was pretty safe in those days, especially up there."

Known for his tireless work ethic, Clarke credited the man who made the biggest impression on his early hockey career. "I was lucky," he says. "We probably had the best junior coach that maybe ever came out of the West: Pat Ginnell produced

---

7. Just five years later, Bill McIntyre would become Bobby's brother-in-law when Bobby married Sandy McIntyre at City Hall in their new home city—Philadelphia.

8. To give you some perspective, it's roughly 760 miles from Philadelphia to Chicago; the young boys travelled approximately 110 miles farther than that—the equivalent of traveling from Philadelphia to New York City—a large part of it on foot.

more NHL players than anybody, I think. I was 16 or 17, and I just remember that every day he made us *work*—just skate and skate and skate. And just shoot. And just practice hard every single day.

"There were days, you know, where we had trips when—after traveling all night—you'd get off the bus, and your equipment would be frozen, but we'd thaw it out and get on that ice and skate. And we learned that if you were going to have any success, it was because you had to work. And when you do that all day, every day, it's no longer work. It becomes just a routine. Doing it hard every day became normal. It was never hard work. It was just normal—so I think that he produced a lot of great players under that theory."

The next summer of significance in Clarke's life is the same one that took the United States by fire: the iconic summer of 1969. It is not only the summer of Woodstock, but also when Neil Armstrong steps on the moon—the first human being ever to do so—uttering the immortal words: "That's one small step for man, one giant leap for mankind."

It's when the very first U.S. troop withdrawals are made from Vietnam and when one of the most iconic photographs ever is taken: The Beatles, in single file, on a zebra crosswalk on Abbey Road. It's the summer of the Manson murders as well as the Chappaquiddick incident, when Senator Ted Kennedy drives off a bridge on his way home from a party on Chappaquiddick Island, Massachusetts. Mary Jo Kopechne, a former campaign aide to his brother, dies in the early morning hours of July 19th in the submerged car, causing years of controversy and speculation as to whether or not he is responsible.

And Bobby Clarke is drafted by the Flyers from the Flin Flon Bombers, where, during his 1,144 games played, he accrued 1,210 points (358 goals and 852 assists) and 1,453 penalty minutes.

"Where we were at the time [junior hockey], pro hockey was so far away," he recalls. "It was in our thoughts, probably; I mean, I grew up my whole life wanting to win the Stanley Cup. But we had no idea what pro hockey was *really* all about. The most we were doing was trying to be good junior players.

"I was in the first full draft that they [the NHL] had, and it really wasn't that big of a deal at the time. A part-time scout called me up and told me I'd been drafted by the Flyers, and I didn't really have any clue what that meant other than I was going to go to training camp. And you never went to training camp with a contract. You always went unsigned. You just showed up at camp and waited to see what happened. And camps in those days were a month or even six weeks. Camp was a long time. You'd go twice a day, practicing and stuff, but you still didn't really know if you were good enough to play [in the NHL], and you didn't know what they were thinking about you or anything. You just went out there and did it. You just played hockey [and let the chips fall as they may]."

But of course he made it. On October 11, 1969, Clarke made his NHL debut wearing his No. 16 jersey[9] and recorded his first point (an assist) just 11 days later against the Maple Leafs, and his first NHL goal on October 30 against the Rangers.

Clarke's first impressions of Philly are understandable: "It was intimidating: the size of the city, the number of cars, and the amount of people," he says. "The sheer size of the rink, the size of the Spectrum was just overwhelming for most of the first year....You know, you just go to the rink and play the game, and go to a diner and eat afterward....You didn't really have much of a social life. You didn't know where to go or how to get there....Looking back, it was probably a good thing—all we did was play hockey."

Right from the start, however, Clarke was an enigma: "When I first broke in, those were the days when players didn't come out of junior hockey and come to the NHL; they mostly all went to the minors, and I happened to come right to the NHL from junior hockey."

He also apparently was gullible. "One of our defenseman— who I thought of as old at the time but was probably only 30 or so—he told me: 'Rookie: you carry my bags.' So whenever we went on the road, I used to always have to carry his bags for him. I'd take them to his room and drop 'em off," Clarke says.

---

9. Clarke wore No. 16 throughout his entire NHL career with the exception of two games during the 1980–81 season when, prior to a road trip, it was discovered that his jersey had been stolen. For the next two games, he wore the only other jersey available: No. 36.

"I was the only first-year pro on the team. I didn't have anyone to tell me any different. So I hauled his bags as well as my own, just hauled them around day after day from city to city…for the first year. I just thought that, you know, 'I guess that's what rookies do.' Who was I to argue? I didn't know any different. It doesn't happen that way anymore and probably never happened that way *before* either, but I didn't know any different."

Clarke's favorite hockey memories are of winning the Cup twice, of course, and winning the Summit Series in 1972 when Canada defeated the Russians, and Clarke won Team Canada MVP in Game 1 of the series.

"It was the first time Canada used professional players on a national team," he says. "They took 32 players to camp. I was 22 years old, the youngest player, and I was also the last choice; a Ranger had been asked but turned it down. So it was just my good fortune. It was unique, exhilarating, and one of the high-lights of my career."

Stanley Cup winner and former Flyers coach Wayne Cashman observed at the time, "There were guys on Team Canada who took their game to new heights in that series. A perfect example would be Bobby Clarke."

The thing most people remember about this series is simply known as "The Tap" or "The Slash," when Clarke laid a two-handed slash against the already sore ankle of Valeri Kharlamov, the Soviets' top player, causing him to miss the seventh game and be virtually ineffective in the eighth.

But the hullabaloo surrounding the move baffles Clarke. When asked about it, he says simply: "If I hadn't learned to lay a two-hander once in a while, I would've never left Flin Flon."

When controversy arose, Team Canada assistant coach John Ferguson rushed to Clarke's defense and insisted it was he who orchestrated the slash, not Clarke. "I called him [Clarke] over to the bench, looked over at Kharlamov and said, 'I think he needs a tap on the ankle.' I didn't think twice about it. It was 'us versus THEM.' And Kharlamov was killing us. I mean somebody had to do it."

Clarke, however, says: "He [Ferguson] was doing what a good coach does. He was taking the heat off of one of his players. But he didn't need to. It [the controversy] didn't bother me. It was the right thing to do at the time. The same people that were glad when it happened were the same ones criticizing it years later. Nobody said a word about it for the longest time. Then, all of a sudden, years and years go by, and people got politically correct, and it became a controversy. But I have no regrets."

Clarke's fabled career includes becoming the youngest team captain in NHL history at the time (age 23), the first Flyer to ever win an NHL award[10], and the first player from an expansion team to score more than 100 points in a season. He played in eight NHL All-Star Games and holds eight first-place records with the Flyers: most points (1,210), most assists (852), most

---

10. Bill Masterton Memorial Trophy.

games played (1,144), plus/minus (+506), shorthanded goals (32), most playoff games played (136), most playoff points (119), and most playoff assists (77). In addition, he was appointed an Officer of the Order of Canada[11] and is a member of the Hockey Hall of Fame, Canada's Sports Hall of Fame, the Philadelphia Flyers Hall of Fame, the Manitoba Hockey Hall of Fame, and the Philadelphia Sports Hall of Fame.

He was also the recipient of Brownridge Trophy[12], the Class Guy Award[13], the Frank J. Selke Trophy[14], Hart Memorial Trophy[15] (three times), Lester B. Pearson Award[16], Lester Patrick Trophy[17], Lionel Conacher Award[18], and the Lou Marsh Trophy[19].

Although Clarke isn't much for accolades, when pressed about which award has meant the most to him, he claimed two: "The Pearson MVP award because it's voted on by the players, and it's pretty special for myself or any player."

The other?

---

11. A Canadian national order, the second highest honor for merit second only to membership in the Order of Merit.

12. Awarded to the top scorer of the Western Hockey League. It has since been renamed the Bob Clarke Trophy.

13. A Flyers team award.

14. Awarded annually to the NHL forward who demonstrates the most skill in the defensive component of the game.

15. Originally known as the Hart Trophy, the oldest and most prestigious individual award in hockey is awarded annually to the "player adjudged most valuable to his team."

"The Selke award because [of the fact that] I'd always been a big scorer, being named the best defensive [forward] player in the game....Well, it told me I was a pretty complete hockey player. And that was really gratifying."

———

When asked, Clarke was very hesitant to give advice to anyone, whether to kids or their parents attempting to guide them.

After a gargantuan pause, he says: "I guess I would give the same advice I used [when dealing] with my own kids, and that's just keep your mouth shut and watch them play. Kids will figure out on their own how much they like a sport, how hard they'll want to compete. All that happens when parents start yelling and hollering is that the kids get embarrassed, and they're made to feel uncomfortable...and is that really what you want, as a parent? Of course not.

---

16. Now known as the Ted Lindsay Award, awarded annually to the NHL's most outstanding player in the regular season as judged by the members of the NHL Players Association.

17. The Lester Patrick Trophy has been presented by the NHL and USA Hockey to honor a recipient's contribution to ice hockey in the United States. It is considered a non-NHL trophy because it may be awarded to players, coaches, officials, and other personnel outside the NHL.

18. An annual award given to Canada's male athlete of the year.

19. Awarded to Canada's Top Athlete of the Year, professional or amateur.

"I'm a big believer in the kids. Let the coaches work with them and let them figure things out on their own. You can help kids and teach them, but they've got to figure out competition, whether they like it or not, how important it is to them, how much they want to practice. You can't do it for them. And if they want to be successful, they'll figure it out. If they want it, they'll all need coaching, they'll all need guidance and rules...but they also have the need of figuring sports out for themselves."

When asked if he has any funny locker room stories, Clarke, a well-known prankster, offers up one of his famous impish grins and chuckles: "I've got millions."

After such an illustrious career, both on the ice and off[20], is it possible that he has any regrets, anything he'd go back and change?

He grows a bit wistful at this, and...after a long pause...he says, "I'd just like one more shift."

---

20. During his 23 seasons as GM (for the Flyers, North Stars, and Panthers), Clarke reached the Stanley Cup Finals four times, and in his first year in the dual role as starting center and Flyers assistant coach in 1979–80, the team had an unbeaten streak of 35 games: not only the longest in NHL history but the longest in North American professional sports history.

CHAPTER 3

BOB KELLY

Born in 1950 in Port Credit, Ontario, Bob Kelly first learned to skate when he was three and a half years old. "We lived right on the Port Credit River, and the rivers up there would freeze all the time," Kelly says. "So that's where I started skating. My dad would go out and test the ice to make sure it was solid, and then I would skate with my mom and sister. You'd skate and play in the snow. We didn't have a whole lot of neighbors. We were kind of isolated where we were, and so it wasn't until later on—when I was six and seven—once I was in school [that I started playing hockey]. And then you've got all the kids out on the river, and everybody's playing hockey because none of the other sports existed. There were no gadgets to play with, to entertain yourself with. So it was all about skating and the snow sports.

"Because of the weather and climate, basically my life in Port Credit for nine months of the year consisted of going to school and playing hockey. Back then, where we were, there was no football, baseball, basketball, soccer…nobody played that stuff. So basically you played street hockey or ice hockey. Then, the other three months of the year, I would be down on my uncle's farm working all summer long. And that was my idea of enjoyment and relaxation: working on the farm.

"It never occurred to me that I could make it [play pro hockey] whatsoever. Coming through Port Credit, basically there was another kid in town, and we were considered 'the stars.' We'd usually get about four or five goals a game…and then they put me in the MTHL [Metro Toronto Hockey League], which would basically be like going from a house league to the best of all-surrounding-Toronto. And I have to thank my coach for hanging in with me…because at that point, my confidence was shattered; I couldn't do nothing with the puck. People were running over me, flattening me.…My skill had evaporated, and it took me about three and a half weeks to get my confidence back. But at that point, if they had cut me, I would've probably been done [with hockey forever]. But they hung in with me, and I just got the opportunity to make it into Junior B."

———

The year is 1967.

The year the Philadelphia 76ers won in six games against the San Francisco Warriors to become the NBA Champions, as well as the year Muhammad Ali was stripped of his World Heavyweight Champion titles and was banned from boxing for his refusal to be inducted into the U.S. Army.

It's also the year of the infamous Ice Bowl, a grudge match

between the Green Bay Packers and Dallas Cowboys. This match up was not only the 35th championship game in NFL history but—due to a combination of the horrific conditions and the game's competitiveness—the Ice Bowl is considered one of the greatest games in NFL history. A rematch of the 1966 NFL title game, this faceoff would pit two future Hall of Fame coaches against each other: Tom Landry for the Cowboys and Vince Lombardi for the Packers, marking the end of one era and the beginning of another.

During 1967 Bob Kelly, then 17, finds himself part of a five-for-one trade that would change his life.

The deal sent Kelly to a rather prestigious major junior club—the Oshawa Generals of the then-OHA (Ontario Hockey Association). Although he'd been a reliable offensive player previously, it was in Oshawa that Kelly quickly established himself as one of the toughest players, knowing not only how to deliver a fierce forecheck but also when to drop his gloves and let the windmill loose.

"I can honestly say I never lost a fight in junior," he recalls. "I went right into Junior A and also went back to school… because I had quit school…and you just prayed for a draft. I mean, you don't know how good you are. Back in those days there wasn't a lot of communication about how well you're doing. It's not like it is today."

As it turned out—on the heels of his second OHA season where he recorded 117 penalty minutes and averaged close to a

point per game (52 points in 53 games, including 21 goals)—
Kelly was drafted by Philadelphia in the third round and 32nd
overall. "All the older guys said, 'Where the hell is Philadelphia?'"
he says. "I mean, I'd never been farther south than Buffalo. It
sounds goofy, but you just didn't venture into the States. Travel,
communication…it wasn't like how it is today."

Another thing that was very different back then was the
draft itself.

"All we knew was the date of the draft, and you just waited
for your phone to ring. If it didn't ring, 'See ya later,'" he said. But
of course he did get the call for which so many young Canadian
men prayed. "I was very excited, very thrilled," he says, "and
again, not really knowing what you were getting yourself into
because there wasn't the hype around it that there is today."

Although relatively few people expected Kelly to make the
big club right away, Kelly holds the impressive distinction of
never having played in the minors. "I played one exhibition
game as a Quebec Ace playing against the Montreal Voyageurs,
and then the Montreal Canadiens played the Flyers in Montreal
the night after us," he says. "I rode back in the bus to Quebec
City, and Vic Stasiuk[21] called me at three o'clock in the morning
and he goes, 'You're dressing today against Montreal.'

---

21. A left-winger who played for the Blackhawks, Red Wings, and Bruins,
Vic Stasiuk won three Stanley Cups with Detroit and recorded 183 goals and 254
assists in the 745 games of his NHL career. After retiring he coached the Flyers,
the now-defunct California Golden Seals, and Vancouver Canucks.

"As we all know—the Original Six teams—we could pretty well name all the players…so to be on the ice with [Jean] Beliveau…and all those guys…it was just outstanding. So my first game, I survived all right. Then Game 2 was Detroit. So in comes Gordie Howe, [Alex] Delvecchio, all those guys, and I survived *that* night without too many elbows. And then the third game I played was against Boston, who'd just won the Cup. So it's [Phil] Esposito, [Ken] Hodge…and so that was my starting three games [in the NHL], and I survived those and you know, from there I got to hang around for a while."

An incident during Kelly's rookie year is noted in hockey folklore—including several books—as one of the most elaborate practical jokes of all time, an initiation ritual now known simply as "the snipe hunt."

Knowing Kelly was a hunting enthusiast, the veterans on the team led by Ed Van Impe told Kelly stories about all the fun they'd been having "snipe" hunting, creating a story about a regional bird that no one actually hunts, though Kelly was none-the-wiser.

"They knew I loved to hunt. So I'd say, 'I hear you guys are going hunting'—I mean, they'd talk about it enough to just make me salivate," Kelly says. "And they'd say, 'Nah, you can't come, kid. Ya can't come. No rookies allowed. It's for us only.'"

But just like on the ice, Kelly was not easily deterred.

"What's a snipe?" he asked.

And Van Impe explained: "They're sort of like pigeons."

Kelly asked if they were edible.

"Only the breasts," Van Impe quipped. "My wife cooks them in a wine sauce, and are they ever delicious!"

After more than a month of Kelly begging to come along, Van Impe said he'd consider making an exception to the "no-rookies rule," and during the next few days, the guys —all in on the joke, of course—schooled Kelly in the art of snipe hunting. From practicing snipe calls, to teaching him how to flush out snipes by beating the bushes with long poles, to shining a flash-light on them when they took flight (explaining that the birds would panic and get confused, allowing the hunters the chance to catch them in fishing nets), Kelly bought every angle of the ruse: hook, line, and sinker.

Taking the joke one (huge) step further, Van Impe arranged with friends in the Delaware County police department to arrest Kelly for "Hunting snipe without a license in a snipe preserve." They even arranged for a stern justice of the peace to scare Kelly into thinking he was going to jail.

Finally—just as real panic began to set in—his new team-mates appeared in the courtroom and let him off the hook.

A well-known prankster himself, Kelly had to laugh.

"Instead of getting your head buzzed or Atomic Balm shoved all over your body or other situations that could occur… it was just another initiation onto the team. So for them to go to the lengths they did to put that together.…I mean, [as a rookie] it's acceptance that you want, of course. So they set it up, and that was better than having my head shaved," he says.

But being a rookie wasn't all fun and games.

There was no guarantee after all that just because you'd made the team that you would have an NHL career.

"Coming here next to Clarkie [Bobby Clarke], who was the first guy to make out it of junior, and I technically was the second guy," Kelly remembers. "We were roommates, and I got to play on his line with Louie Morrison. And we were under the tutelage of all the older guys. I mean, we were young kids—it was Clarkie's second year, my first year—and just because you made it, didn't mean you'd stay. I mean, you just didn't know how long you would stick [in the NHL]."

But of course they both did. Kelly explained his theory as to why: "We [Clarke and Kelly] supplied an element that the Flyers organization was looking for because they were getting pushed around by St. Louis, Boston," he says. "So then we really started to complement it with Schultzy [Dave Schultz] and the Bird [Don Saleski], and we picked the Moose [Andre Dupont] up… and Freddy [Shero] changed the composure of the team there a bit. So probably the way I played allowed me to stay, which was good because we had a lot of smaller guys, so it gave me the opportunity to get into some scuffles and all that."

A poster boy for the ferocious Broad Street Bullies, Bob "the Hound" Kelly finished his career with 1,454 well-earned penalty minutes.

He recalls his most memorable fight: "I had lots of fights, but probably the one that's funny—because we played together later[22]—was Moose Dupont. My mom called the Moose "the Boxcar" because he was 255 pounds, and he was mean and nasty and big. We had a bench-clearing brawl in Oshawa [Ontario], and Moose fought about two guys. And I turn around toward the end of the brawl, and Moose is on his knees looking up at me, and his big head is just sitting there. And I said to myself, 'You gotta hit it.' So I hit him in the head, and we all got thrown out of the game. I'm in and showered and [outside of the locker rooms], I'm walking down the hallway, and this door comes flying open—you couldn't have timed it better—and Moose is spitting blood and crap out of his face, his mouth, his nose, and he goes, 'Good fight. We go again in Montreal.'

"And I go, 'Oh yeah, Moose, I can't wait for that to happen.' The next game in Montreal, the crowd's huge—over 21,000 for a junior game—and there's seven of us sitting on the bench. And we were getting pelted with ice cream, beer, you name it… it only took about a minute or so to get into the first brawl," he says. "And they had some other guys that could fight there pretty good, too. So looking back, that was probably my most memorable fight because the Moose and I ended up playing together."

Another favorite memory for Kelly happened on the road. "Probably the one that's the funniest was 'the duck massacre' in

---

22. Bob Kelly and Andre Dupont would end up being teammates on the Flyers from 1972–73 until 1979–1980.

Boston, during the playoffs. At the time for whatever reason, there were a plethora of ducks from where we were to where we had to get to, and unfortunately for them, they were in between. So somehow I managed to get a duck and I also managed to get a key to [Bobby] Clarkie's hotel room. You have to understand, Clarkie would pee in shampoo bottles, cut ties, cut up shoes.... He was an awful man," he jokes. "And so, as a bit of a payback, I take this dead duck and propped him up on Clarkie's pillow and I put a cigar in his mouth and gave him a little wing span," he says. "As it turned out, we didn't have to leave till the next afternoon, so I come back to the hotel, go to bed, fall asleep, and when it was time to go, just got up, and kinda threw all my stuff together and got going. Back then we all carried leather bags that went over your shoulder, and as I'm going along, I'm looking at my bag and thinking, 'What the heck smells? Something smells in here.' Well, your dad [Clarke] had snuck back into my room while I was sleeping and tucked the duck in my leather bag. So there's a dead duck in my bag, and it didn't smell very good," he laughs. "There were ducks put in the ice machine [of the hotel]; they were hanging over the doors. They were everywhere. It was crazy."

Fred Shero deserves the credit for seeing something in Kelly that could be more valuable to the Flyers than just points. He saw Kelly's ability to deliver ferocious forechecks and win fights and used him accordingly. In fact, Shero most famously said, "If Bob Kelly scores 20 goals, I'm not using him properly." However, while Kelly is best known for being an enforcer, he still made offensive contributions as well, recording 362 points (154 goals and 208 assists) in 837 games played. A well-rounded player who spent a solid decade in the NHL, any guidance Kelly has to offer should be noted, despite however reluctant he was to give it.

"Well, my first piece of advice to parents is that they should observe and just shut up," Kelly says. "And by saying that, it's not disrespectful…but as soon as a kid puts on a pair of skates or throws a baseball or football, all of a sudden [some parents believe] their kid is going to the Hall of Fame. They're gonna make it…and that's kind of a big rejection when things don't happen. And you burn your kid out to where he doesn't want to participate anymore because you've been trying to push him too hard, and the coaches push him hard, and he's not really enjoying it that much. And I think you have to have a balance in there where you get enjoyment out of watching your kid play at whatever level they play at—and you obviously try to give them the option to better themselves by going to summer camps or whatever. But you really need to understand the mission statement of the team they're playing on. What's the real focus here? Are we here to win; are we here to compete? Are we here to win at all costs? So I think you gotta understand the mission statement and understand the talent level your child is playing at and evaluate things from there. I mean, most kids aren't going to make it. And some think they can go out there and score some goals during a game, and that's it. What they don't understand is that you have to shoot hundreds of pucks all day long. You gotta skate and work on your weaknesses… there's a reason why there's only so many people that make it. I mean, when we played there were only six teams to start, and it was a North American sport with only three or four Americans in it. Now there's 30 teams, and it's a worldwide sport. So the competition is even steeper yet.

"I always ask my kids, 'Hey, are you having fun? Is this what you want to do?' An example is my daughter Lindsay, who's 12 now. I had her in karate for three years, and she was really doing well. The problem was to do any better, she would have to go to the next level, which meant total commitment. It meant four to five days a week at least, and she wasn't enjoying it enough to make that commitment. If she had wanted to take that opportunity to go further in that sport or any other, we would've supported her, of course. But she didn't, and we supported her decision. So I think you just have to feel your kid out. If it's a chore to go [and play a sport], then it's not fun. If they don't want to go, that's not where they need to be."

But it was always fun for Kelly, and when he looks back, he has two shining moments that make him proud: "The first thing is just to have made it in the National Hockey League. Being drafted and being able to stick and make it—and be a contributor—staying in one city for 10 years," he says. "I was pretty happy about that. Obviously you'd always like it to be a little longer, but 10 years was a good run. Probably my second most would be winning the Cup. When you're a team player, you accept whatever role you're given and you just go out and do it. When I got knocked out in that Rangers series in the first Stanley Cup run, I never got to play against Boston. Five of us went down during that series: obviously Barry Ashbee's eye, Dorny [Gary Dornhoefer] with his legs, and I ended up getting my knee ripped up, and so I couldn't finish that Boston series. So if you're not in that locker room bleeding, going through the pain and agony, and achieving on the road and stuff like that, then you don't feel part of it. So because I scored the game-winning goal in the Buffalo series… it had no real relevance to me personally…[what mattered] was going start to finish [with the team], going the distance. I got to play and contribute till the end of the series. There were a lot of goals that were important throughout. So just being able to go the whole distance and win the Cup. That's what's most important to me."

CHAPTER 4

BILLY BARBER

Located in the Saint Lawrence Lowlands of southwestern Ontario, the city of Kitchener was founded in 1784 when land was given to the Six Nations (Iroquois) by the British as a gift for their allegiance during the American Revolution. From 1796 to 1798, the Six Nations sold about 15 percent of this land to a Loyalist by the name of Colonel Richard Beasley. Though remote, the property was of great interest to German Mennonite farming families from Pennsylvania, who eventually migrated there.

It's also where Billy Barber caught the eye of pro scouts when he centered on a line with Jerry Byers and Al Blanchard while playing for the Kitchener Rangers of the OHA (Ontario Hockey Association), a fierce, top-scoring line that led to all three being drafted high into the NHL.[23]

———

The year is 1972.

---

23. Billy Barber ultimately was the only one of the three to make a significant impact in the NHL.

It's the year the Oakland Athletics win their first World Championship since the team was based in Philadelphia in 1930, as well as the year Paul Henderson scores the "Goal of the Century" to give Canada the win in the Summit Series, the first ever hockey showdown between Canada and the Soviet Union.

It is also the year of the Immaculate Reception when, during the final seconds of the first Pittsburgh Steelers playoff game in 25 years (and the franchise's first playoff win), rookie Franco Harris salvaged and converted a deflected pass by Terry Bradshaw into a touchdown—in what has been called the greatest play in NFL history—to beat the Oakland Raiders 13–7.

And Billy Barber would find himself playing on another formidable line, this time alongside Bobby Clarke and Reggie Leach: the famous LCB (Leach, Clarke, Barber) line.

"I was very proud and honored to be drafted. I was fortunate where I was taken in the draft, in the first round," he says. "I went through Montreal's fingers and got to Philly. I was very, very pleased with that because I wanted to play in the NHL right away and I don't know if I would have had that opportunity in Montreal. They had three picks in that little window that was open between picks four and eight, and I went seven and I was so excited and honored. When you pay the price at a young age, leaving home, going to school in another area, boarding with other families, and doing all that kind of stuff just so you could play…you just hoped one day you could make it. So getting drafted was a dream come true."

But let's go back to when it all began, when Billy is four years old, just learning to skate.

"For the first two or three years [after learning to skate], we just played pond hockey, all age groups from about six years old up to about 13 years old," Barber says. "We all started on a pond, not in an official rink. We were fortunate enough in a small community to even have a rink built. We didn't have any other distractions as far as sports went; hockey was the only sport. None of us really had the opportunity to play indoors or on artificial ice. Everything was done outside, and the winters were cold enough that we would get ice usually in the middle of November right on through to the middle of March. I was kind of spoiled later on in the early '60s when we had an outdoor rink right next to the house. So we got to skate and play every day.

"Organized hockey came when I was around seven years old. We formed a team and began playing official games. The good part about coming from a very small community is that you usually had a total of eight players—nine with the goaltender—and we usually only had two guys on defense. Two lines were all we ever had. I was fortunate enough to be one of the guys on defense, where we never came off the ice in a tournament or a game, and it gave you all the ice time you could handle."

Barber credited two entities as having the greatest impact on his desire to play hockey at an early age.

First, his brothers.

"I had two older brothers, and we all played as a family," he says. "There were five of us in total. They were very influential from a very young age. It just kind of went that way where the oldest was involved in hockey, and you just kind of followed the trend. You go with them to the ice rink and skate and play and have fun."

The second, *Hockey Night in Canada*.

"I remember watching *Hockey Night in Canada* as an eight- or nine-year-old," Barber says. "And your dreams just start to fly from there. I remember thinking, 'There's where I'd like to be.' My parents used to go out every Saturday night, and *Hockey Night in Canada* started at 8 PM. They'd leave us boys behind, and it was a ritual: every Saturday night guaranteed, we were gathered around the TV watching....It was everything as a young boy to sit and cheer for your favorite team, and at that time it was the Original Six. I remember watching Gordie Howe and Bobby Hull. It was something we looked forward to all week. Usually all day on Saturday, we'd be on the ice the whole day. Then Saturday night we'd be watching the stars play. It was bred in us."

After being drafted, Barber played just 11 games with the Richmond Robins[24] before being called up and converted from center to left wing by coach Fred Shero. Barber went on to

---

24. The Flyers' AHL affiliate at the time.

record 64 points (30 goals and 34 assists) and was a contender for the Calder Memorial Trophy for Rookie of the Year.

"From my situation, coming in as a young kid, Fred Shero was a great fit for me because he gave me every opportunity to play, and I'm very grateful for that," Barber says. "I think he was a great man that was maybe a little different from the other coaches, but he got the best out of his players. He had that personality about him. Fred Shero was such a great mix for our hockey team."

During his 12 years with the Flyers, Barber scored a minimum of 20 goals every season, with his best being the 1975–76 season, when he recorded 50 goals and 62 assists. He also contributed six goals to their successful Cup run in 1975.

Serving as a key element during the Flyers' 35-game unbeaten streak, Barber helped the Flyers reach the 1980 Stanley Cup Finals with several crucial goals against the Rangers and Minnesota North Stars.

One of his most memorable goals, however, came during the 1976 Canada Cup. Team Canada was trailing Czechoslovakia in the Final, and Barber scored to send the game into overtime, which led to a Team Canada victory.

Known as a consistent playmaker, go-to goal scorer, and one who could hold his own defensively, Barber says, "I want to be remembered as being capable of doing my job day in and day out, not just as a goal scorer but as a good all-around player for every kind of situation."

A team leader, Barber still holds the Flyers' regular season scoring record with 420 goals and is tied with Rick MacLeish for the most playoff goals with 53. "From a leadership standpoint, I look at Clarkie, Eddie Van Impe, Barry Ashbee," Barber says. "They took their jobs very seriously and the responsibility aspect of coming in and competing hard, all the preparation that goes into playing the very best you can play and trying to win....I found myself around some great people, and I'm very fortunate for that."

Although they were serious on the ice, this Flyers team loved to let loose off the ice as well. When asked about a funny prank-pulling story, he says: "Oh boy," and laughs. "There were a lot of them. I think some of the funniest ones happened when a pretty big war got started with the destroying of cowboy boots and clothing. It got so bad—it became such a problem amongst the team that Fred Shero had to step in and put an end to it. I'll never forget. We were on the road on a one-game road trip to Minneapolis, and one of the guys—the pant leg of his suit had been cut. And when you go on a one-game road trip, you didn't pack a whole lot...you just kind of wore what was on your back. And we flew commercial back then. So imagine seeing a guy coming through the airport wearing a pair of pants with one whole leg missing. Pretty humorous...for the rest of us at least."

Barber captained the Flyers in the 1981–82 season as well as part of the following one before retiring prematurely due to an ongoing knee injury.

"We played a lot of hockey. When you go to the Finals so many times—three in a row—the amount of hockey that's played…you know I felt frustrated the last two years of my career where I wasn't getting a full season in, and I had complications. It was difficult. And after retiring—you're always wondering what it would have been like to continue on—at maybe a far lesser role or changing your position to continue to play but still be able to be part of the Flyers. It's very difficult, but I got over it because when you're not 100 percent, you don't want to leave the game with a bad taste in your mouth in the sense that you weren't producing and helping your team win. So I felt that maybe this is the way it should be, 'Leave while you can and keep the good memories rather than try to hang on and keep getting hurt—and hurting the team—down the line.'"

After retiring in 1984, Barber embarked on a coaching career that began with the Hershey Bears and led to the Flyers, where he was an assistant coach for three years. He was then named head coach of the Phantoms, the Flyers' new AHL affiliate, during their inaugural season in 1996.

Just two years later, under Barber's direction, they became champions.

———

The year 1998 was a major one for hockey.

It was the final season for the Toronto Maple Leafs at Maple

Leaf Gardens before they moved to the Air Canada Centre.

During the XVIII Olympic Winter Games held in Nagano, Japan, players from the NHL were able to compete in men's ice hockey due to a three-week suspension of the NHL season, while women's ice hockey debuted with the United States[25] beating Canada 3–1 for the gold medal.

And, just as in their inaugural season, the Phantoms again finished first overall with 106 points and, again, Peter White took home the Sollenberger Trophy as the League's top scorer with another 105-point season.

On June 10 before a crowd of 17,380 (the club's ninth sellout of the year) the Phantoms defeated the Saint John Flames, 6–1, in Game 6 bolstered by the spectacular goaltending of Neil Little[26]. That set the stage for team captain John Stevens[27] and his teammates to parade the Calder Cup around the same ice as the Flyers had skated their first Stanley Cup 24 years earlier.

After such an impressive run, Barber was named Flyers head coach and was honored with the Jack Adams Award as Coach of the Year in 2001.

---

25. United States went undefeated in the women's tournament.

26. Little allowed just 48 postseason goals and was on his way to a 15–5 playoff record.

27. John Stevens also won Calder Cups with Hershey in 1988 and Springfield in 1991 and would coach the Phantoms to another title in 2005. He was head coach of the Flyers for three-plus seasons and is currently an assistant coach with the L.A. Kings.

In Barber's tenure as a coach in both the AHL and NHL, he coached 472 games, tallying 266 wins, 141 losses, and 55 ties. So perhaps it would be prudent to heed any advice Coach Barber has to offer.

"Some parents get way too heavily involved. Parents should not live their dreams through their kids. When he or she is a good athlete, and you start pushing them too hard," Barber says, "that just sets you up for failure. I think if a kid is good at a sport…or not so good at a sport…as long as they love playing, that's all that matters.

"What I would say to kids is, 'You need to keep in perspective that this is not professional. This is a hobby, a sport that you like to participate in and be around your friends. But at the same time I would say, 'don't lose sight of your dreams either. Whether or not you're good enough to be recognized in the sports world, just keep it in perspective. First of all, go have fun. Second, be honest. And third, work hard for your team and not for yourself.'

"The most important thing I learned about hockey didn't come from any one coach," he says. "It came from all of them: the importance of playing with honesty and being honest with your teammates."

When asked what he is most proud of during his awesome NHL career, Barber says it's not the personal achievements (such as making an impressive six All-Star appearances). Instead, he says: "It's really hard to pinpoint just one thing. It always seems to be more team-related than individual. The easiest thing [to say] is the

two Stanley Cups because they were two very, very special times.
In any athlete's career, when your team is the best in the league and
you win, it's just very special. I think the game against Boston to
win, the game also in Buffalo to win…those are games that stand
out. If I had to pinpoint any one personal thing, it would be the
year that your dad [Bobby Clarke] and Reggie and I stuck together
as a line—the LCB line—where Reggie had 60-some goals,
and I remember scoring the 50th against Buffalo in the second-
to-last game of the year in Philly.…But really it was our line and

our team. That year I think we had 140-some goals, and for one line, I think even in today's game, some teams would love to have that.

"I think Freddy's saying: 'Win today and you'll walk together forever' is so very true. You look at the Stanley Cup teams, and the guys were so close, and we are to this day. The Flyers Alumni, all the people that are involved…Your dad and I were very fortunate to start and end our career in the same city. It's something to be proud of, something that you work hard to try to do: to stay with one team and to have the loyalty and respect of the fans."

————

During 1990 Bill Barber received induction into the Hockey Hall of Fame, and the Flyers retired his No. 7 jersey on October 7.

"It was a big thrill, for me personally and family-wise," he says. "I couldn't be any more proud or honored. It is an honor and a thrill even to this day. You're mentioned and you might be passed over, and another year goes by. And then something happens in that direction [that you might be inducted]…and then it starts to hit home. You start thinking about the names and the players that have been inducted and you're about to be recognized in that category.…It's a big thrill. And from there I have to once again reflect upon my teammates because again, it is a *team* sport. To have success especially in hockey, you need good people around you. You need good teammates and good management and good ownership. And that's what Philly provided and always *will* provide: Mr. [Ed] Snider and the management, the teams, and the coaches....The Flyers have always done a great job in that area.

"My first impression of Philly was that it was just so big," he says. "When you come from a small area like I did, you just can't believe the size, the number of people....It was an experience within itself. But it grew on all of us as players. We all ended up falling in love with the city and the people who followed us. We just loved our fans. You just can't speak highly enough about South Philly and the city of Philadelphia and their fan base. It's the greatest place in the world to play sports, because if you take your job seriously and you play hard...they love you back."

CHAPTER 5

DAVE SCHULTZ

When one thinks of Philly, some images immediately spring to mind: cheesesteaks, soft pretzels, cream cheese, Tastykake, the Declaration of Independence, the Liberty Bell, Quakers, Ben Franklin.

And when one thinks of the Broad Street Bullies, Dave Schultz is at the top of the list, conjuring images of bare fists—cocked and loaded ready to do some damage—along with a menacing face you wouldn't want to come across in a dark alley.

Dave "the Hammer" Schultz's legacy with the Flyers casts a shadow as wide as a Wildwood beach and as tall as the statue of Billy Penn.

So would it surprise you to learn that Schultzy played only four seasons with the Flyers?

Yes, that's right just four from 1972 to 1976.[28]

A mere 297 games.

Yet he is a permanent fixture in this city, a founding father of the Flyers franchise. Like a tornado, he touched down, made his mark, and moved on. Yet his antics are threaded so deep

---

28. Dave Schultz also played in one game as a rookie in 1971–72.

within the fabric of Philly's sports lore that Betsy Ross might have woven it herself.

"Davey is the player who gave the Broad Street Bullies their personality that the organization carried long after Davey was gone," Bobby Clarke told Philadelphiaflyers.com. "We had good players, but that personality was a big part of our organization."

And those four seasons are nothing to scoff at either. They include winning the Stanley Cup twice, going to the Final for three straight seasons, and beating the Russian Central Red Army team.

When sports fans hear the name "Dave Schultz," the words shy or quiet never come to mind. Except those words are true.

Born in Waldheim, Saskatchewan, Schultz spent the bulk of his childhood moving from farm to farm, town to town with his family.

———

The year is 1953.

It's the year the first color television sets go on sale, when the first Chevrolet Corvette is built in Flint, Michigan, as well as when the Philadelphia stadium, originally called Shibe Park is renamed Connie Mack Stadium.

And Dave Schultz, age four, is first learning to skate.

"I started skating out in front of the house on the farm or on the dugout," he says.

The dugout?

Schultzy says, "A dugout is man-made for water to collect so the cows could drink. They were maybe only four or five or six feet deep, but in the wintertime they'd freeze solid. Basically, wherever there was water that would freeze, we'd skate on it. Thirty or 40 below didn't bother us."

At the age of eight, Dave Schultz began to play organized hockey in 1957.

"We had an outdoor rink," he says. "I was either playing on that, on the frozen road, or we made our own rink in the backyard. Once the snow comes, the roads are ice covered the whole time. It gets packed down, and it was better than playing on gravel. We didn't have pavement back then, at least not in Saskatchewan. We'd just make our own rink. When it snowed you'd just take the snow and plop it over on the other side of the boards, and that's where you'd stand to watch the games when you weren't playing.

"When you're in a town of three or four or five hundred people, most of the kids were bused in from the farm. There were very few kids in town. You got together with your friends, five or six guys max, and you'd just go out and play. All the time. It didn't matter how cold it was. Even when I lived on the farm, and we got bused to town, I could still go public skating. It was about a half-mile walk to the outdoor rink there, and you could go skating there during our noon hour [lunch break at school]."

His first experience playing indoor hockey came about four years after first playing organized hockey. It was also Schultzy's first experience with artificial ice.

"I was a rink rat. Me and my brother and a couple other buddies—that's what we did. We played hockey on the street or on the lake or on the rink. It was something I loved right from the very beginning. The winters are fairly long, and at the school, there was no gymnasium. So you played hockey. Back in those days, we'd go down to the hardware store to watch *Hockey Night in Canada*. We didn't have a TV. It was a different way of life, but we didn't know the difference. There was not much else to do besides play hockey in those small towns, and we loved it.

"My dad was a pretty good hockey player. He was kind of the black sheep of the family," he says. "He liked to go drinking and stuff. But he was a pretty good hockey player, and they had a pretty good team in Waldheim. So my dad used to always tell me: 'Behave. I'll bet you Bobby Orr doesn't go out and drink.' And you know what was interesting? On that note when I was in grade 10, I had to give a speech in school, and there was a big article in a Canadian magazine on Bobby Orr. And I did my speech on Bobby Orr. He was sixteen at the time, and I was fifteen.

"Back in those days, living in a small town, parents would drive you to away games, 5 or 20 miles away to other little towns. But the time and money commitment of today is just so different. Parents today put so much time and money into hockey now. Even with practices, kids have to be driven to practices, and the parents stay there; it's a lot of time spent. Whereas when we were young, we just threw our hockey bags over our shoulders and grabbed our sticks and walked to the rink no matter if it was 20 or 30 below with the wind blowing and howling around....We just went to the rink. And I blame that—the time and money commitment that's so different today. The parents put so much into it, and they want to see their kids get scholarships and that kind of stuff, and they get carried away sometimes. And there's a lot of pressure on the kids. There was never that kind of pressure for me. My dad always told me to work hard and behave yourself and maybe you can go somewhere, but there was never that pressure."

As Schultz grew up, his ability on the ice garnered attention but not for fighting. A solid point producer, Schultz recorded 167 points (85 goals and 82 assists) during his first four seasons.

"In junior I was playing bantam then midget in Lucky Lake. Then we moved back to Rosetown, and I got invited to the Estevan Bruins[29] training camp," he says. "They were a very good team in the Western Canada Hockey League. So that's

---

29. Originally founded as the Humboldt Indians, the team moved to Estevan in 1957 and became a founding member of the Western Hockey League in 1966. They won the President's Cup in 1967–68 and in 1971 moved to New Westminster, British Columbia, where they became the New Westminster Bruins. Today that franchise is the Kamloops Blazers. With the departure of the major junior Bruins, a new Bruins team was founded in Estevan that same year and has played in the SJHL ever since, winning the Saskatchewan Junior Hockey League champions in 1985 and 1999.

when I started playing junior, and three years later I got drafted by the Flyers.

"When you're playing youth hockey, you just play. We loved to play; we loved the competition. When I finally got to junior, the Western Canada Hockey League used overage players that had been outlawed by the CAHA [the Canadian Amateur Hockey Association], and Scotty Munro,[30] who put a lot of players into the NHL, was our coach. And we were all cut from the Estevan Bruins. There were like 20 of us. We got cut and sent to Swift Current. I was on the first team ever of the Swift Current Broncos, and our coach there was a guy named Harvey Roy. And when I got there, I was like a sponge. I wanted to learn everything, not having any idea I'd ever play in the National Hockey League. And I learned a lot from the whole experience, but from him I learned things like how to shake someone's hand, work hard, be a good team player. So I tried hard and scored a lot of goals and from there I got drafted."

During Schultz's three years with the Swift Current Broncos he played in 118 games, tallying 133 points (70 goals and 63 assists) and 203 penalty minutes. He also caught the attention of the Flyers, who drafted him in the fifth round.

---

30. One of the founders of the Western Hockey League, Munro served as the general manager of the Estevan Bruins and later as the head coach and general manager of the Calgary Centennials. The Scotty Munro Memorial Trophy is awarded annually to the regular season champion of the Western Hockey League.

Dave "The Hammer" Schultz was drafted in 1969, after expansion occurred two years earlier.

"The expansion happened in '67, and this was only a couple years later," he says. "Prior to the expansion, if you played for the Estevan Bruins, you were a Boston Bruins property, and that's the way all the junior teams were. You belonged to a specific team. But that all changed when the expansion came. I was aware of the pros a little bit. I knew that a lot of players had gone there, that had played in Estevan, that went on to play in the NHL. So I got home from my summer job and I looked in the newspaper and I saw the draft, and it had the names listed. And that's how I found out I'd been drafted: I read it in the newspaper."

The Flyers acquired Schultz and sent him to the Salem Rebels of the Eastern Hockey League, where over the course of 67 games he recorded 69 points (32 goals and 37 assists) and 356 penalty minutes. And from there the penalties only increased as Schultz learned to fight.[31]

"[Up until the minors] I'd had only two fights in three years. I never really fought till I was 20 years old. The movie

---

31. 382 penalty minutes with the Quebec Aces of the American Hockey League the following year and 392 with the AHL Richmond Robins the year after that.

Slap Shot[32], that's where I started," he jokes. "I got in a couple fights, and it took off from there, big time."

So what was Schultzy's first impression of Philly?

"I was pretty scared," he says. "I'd played in Richmond, Virginia, and Roanoke. I'd had a couple years playing in front of decent crowds, but this was a whole new world."

———

Ranked 10th in the NHL with the most career playoff penalty minutes (412), Schultz was an enforcer. Over the course of his four seasons with the Flyers, he tallied 115 points (51 goals and 64 assists) and a whopping 1,386 penalty minutes. So the reason he acquired the nickname "the Hammer" is not exactly a mystery. But what may be is—who is responsible for actually coining the moniker that's stuck like glue for 40 years?

It was Jack Chevalier, a sportswriter for the *Philadelphia Bulletin*, who is also credited with creating the nickname Broad Street Bullies[33]. Schultz says: "I don't know if it was my first or

---

32. The legendary comedy starring Paul Newman that depicts a minor league hockey team that resorts to violent play to gain popularity in a declining factory town, *Slap Shot* has been named the "Best Guy Movie of All Time" (*Maxim* magazine, 1998), one of the "30 films that changed Men's Lives" (*GQ* magazine, 50th Anniversary Issue, 2007), and "the best hockey film ever made" (*The Hockey News*, 2008), just to name a few. A hilarious portrayal of minor league hockey, *Slap Shot* has stood the test of time as a cult classic since its release in 1977.

second year with the Flyers, but Jack Chevalier—it was after a fight obviously—wrote: 'Schultz sure hammered him,' and that's how that started."

Schultz led the NHL in penalty minutes three times, including setting an NHL record with most penalty minutes in a single season in 1974–75 with 472, a record he still holds to this day.

But he was much more than a pair of taped-up fists ready to swing at whomever was foolish enough to get caught in his crosshairs. Schultz recorded double-digits in goals twice, including a career best of 20 during the 1973–74 season, scored twice against Buffalo in Game 5 of the '75 Final and assisted Bobby Clarke's overtime goal to beat Boston in Game 2 of the '74 Final.

He left his mark on the hockey world in other ways as well. After injuring his wrist in a fight, Schultz put boxing wraps on his hands for protection. The trick worked, and pretty soon the trend caught on. Before long all the enforcers in both the National Hockey League and World Hockey Association were wearing similar hand protection: not to protect an injury but to prevent themselves from injury in a fight. Soon after this trick became popular, both the WHA and NHL passed what became

---

33. During the 1972–73 season, after a brawling victory over the Atlanta Flames, Jack Chevalier wrote: "The image of the fightin' Flyers is spreading gradually around the NHL, and people are dreaming up wild nicknames. They're the Mean Machine, the Bullies of Broad Street and Freddy's Philistines." And thus, the Broad Street Bullies moniker was born.

known as the "Schultz Rule"—thus banning the boxing wraps from professional ice hockey.

Though he played fewer than 300 games with the Flyers, Schultz was inducted into the Flyers Hall of Fame during November 2009, proving to everyone that it's often quality—not quantity—that makes a legend.

CHAPTER 6

PAUL HOLMGREN

The year is 1955 when an on-ice altercation ignites one of the worst incidents of hockey-related violence in history. It leads to a riot at the Forum in Montreal that caused an estimated $100,000 in damages, 37 injuries, and 100 arrests.

Back then Maurice "Rocket" Richard of the Canadiens is considered a hero among French Canadians during a time when they are frequently treated as second-class citizens. Often compared to fellow minority Jackie Robinson of Major League Baseball, Richard was the target of consistent, ruthless harassment by opposing teams—including vicious ethnic slurs—and racks up numerous fines and suspensions for his retaliations.

After receiving five stitches from a high stick to the head delivered by Boston Bruin Hal Laycoe during a game in March 1955, Richard attacks Laycoe with his stick, ultimately breaking it over him before knocking him unconscious.

Subsequent attempts by the Boston police to arrest Richard are thwarted when his fellow teammates bar the door to their locker room.

He *was* punished, however. NHL president Clarence Campbell suspends him for the remainder of the season—including the playoffs—prompting outrage from Montreal fans who think the penalty was too severe. French Canadians in particular feel he is unjustly punished due to his ethnicity, and when Campbell makes an appearance at a game at the Forum three days after the incident, his presence provokes an outrageous melee now known as the Richard Riot.

So perhaps it is fitting that this was the same year notorious fighter and Flyers enforcer Paul Holmgren was born.

Throughout all eight seasons with the Flyers, he was a contributor on offense as well—with career highs in goals (30) and points (65) in a single season—he is likely best known for setting a franchise record for most penalty minutes (1,600).

———

But let's go back to 1957.

It is the year both the Frisbee and Ford Motor Company's Edsel first debut. Dr. Seuss' *The Cat in the Hat* is first published, and *Leave it to Beaver* premieres on television. Elvis Presley, then 22 years old, appears on *The Ed Sullivan Show* for the third and final time and is only shown from the waist up before going on to purchase Graceland that same year for $100,000.

And in St. Paul, Minnesota, Paul Holmgren is two years old and first learning how to skate.

Paul's dad, a farmer from Wisconsin, owned a plot of land. "In the summertime it was a big garden, and in the wintertime, he flooded it, and everyone in the neighborhood used to come and skate there. And that's where I learned to skate, on that little frozen patch of land right next door to the house I grew up in," he recalls. "That's my earliest memory."

Also about three blocks away was the playground where Paul—along with his siblings and friends—often played. "The roads were frozen over, and the snowplows were not doing a very good job in those days," he recalls. "So we could literally skate from our house up to the playground where there was a great big general rink where anybody could go out and skate. And then they had two hockey rinks where there were always two games going on. So you could jump in and play.

"I don't remember skating indoors until I was a bantam [about 13 or 14 years old]. All my hockey growing up was outdoors. And it didn't matter if it was 20 below or 20 above, we were outdoors playing all the time—a lot of good memories," he says.

The youngest of four kids, Paul's first experience with organized hockey was at the peewee level. "I have a brother who's just 15 months older, and we played on the same teams all the time growing up," Holmgren says. "Whether it was baseball, football, or hockey, we were always on the same team...and we always had good teams. Our hockey team was always one of the better teams in the area, and actually, a lot of the guys from that time went on to play on our high school team—we made it to the state tournament two years in a row. Getting to play together was really special."

Holmgren said he never really thought much about playing pro hockey. "It was a far-fetched idea I never even thought of," he said quite matter-of-factly. And so in 1974–75, he found himself playing at the University of Minnesota. "It was very important for my parents that I go to college and try to get a degree. I only stayed in college one year and then turned pro after it, but none of those aspirations ever came to my mind even after the season, and then all of sudden I started getting calls. That year I was drafted by both the World Hockey Association [WHA] and the Flyers. So the wheels starting turning for me… but up until that point I had no real aspirations of playing pro."

––––––

34. Hoping to follow in the footsteps of Moses Malone a year after the ABA's Utah Stars plucked him right out of a Virginia high school, an 18-year-old Dawkins renounced his college eligibility and applied for the 1975 NBA Draft as a hardship candidate. The Sixers made him the fifth overall pick (behind David Thompson, David Meyers, Marvin Webster, and Alvan Adams) believing like so many others that with his size, speed, and touch, Dawkins would take over the league. However, they quickly found he was a raw talent that needed time to develop, and it took two years before he earned a regular spot on the roster.

He eventually found his groove and would go on to play 14 seasons in the NBA with the Sixers, the New Jersey Nets, the Detroit Pistons, and Utah Jazz, averaging double figures in scoring nine times—often ranking among the league leaders in field-goal percentage—and playing in the NBA Finals three times as a Sixer.

Nicknamed "Chocolate Thunder" for his powerful dunks, which led the NBA to adopt breakaway rims due to him shattering the backboard on two occasions in 1979, Dawkins set an NBA record for fouls in a season (386 in 1983–84) and never quite lived up to the expectations that had been heaped upon him when he was drafted out of high school.

The year is 1975.

In baseball the Cincinnati Reds win 4–3 against the Boston Red Sox, which is often described as one of the most memorable World Series of all time.

In basketball the 76ers select Darryl Dawkins, who becomes the second NBA player drafted straight out of high school[34]. College coaching legend John Wooden leads his UCLA squad to victory 92–85 against Kentucky in the in what would be Wooden's[35] final game as UCLA coach.

---

35. Nicknamed the "Wizard of Westwood", John Wooden was an American basketball player and coach.

As a player he won a national championship at Purdue and was the first ever to be named an All-American three times.

During his tenure as UCLA head coach, Wooden gained lasting fame by winning 620 games in 27 seasons and 10 NCAA titles during his last 12 seasons, including seven in a row from 1967 to 1973, an unprecedented feat. His UCLA teams also had a record winning streak of 88 games, four perfect 30–0 seasons, 38 straight wins in NCAA Tournaments, and 98 straight home game wins at Pauley Pavilion.

Named NCAA College Basketball's Coach of the Year seven times, he was named the Henry Iba Award USBWA College Basketball Coach of the Year award in 1967, and just five years later shared *Sports Illustrated* magazine's "Sportsman of the Year" award with Billie Jean King.

Revered and beloved by his former players, such as Kareem Abdul-Jabbar and Bill Walton, Wooden was renowned for his short, simple inspirational messages to his players, including his "Pyramid of Success" messages that were often were directed at how to be a success in life as well as in basketball.

Wooden was named a member of the Basketball Hall of Fame as a player (inducted in 1961) and as a coach (in 1973), the first person ever to be enshrined in both categories. (Only Lenny Wilkens and Bill Sharman have since had the same honor).

And Paul Homlgren begins his professional hockey career—one that had a bit of a rocky start.

Though Holmgren was selected by the Edmonton Oilers 67th overall in the 1974 WHA Amateur Draft, he never played for them, as his WHA rights were traded to the Minnesota Fighting Saints. So he went to play in his home state—only to leave the team three days before it folded due to financial problems—and went on to be selected by the Philadelphia Flyers 108th overall in the amateur draft of that same year. He signed with the Flyers shortly after and made his NHL debut a month later.

Surprisingly, Holmgren was never a fighter until *after* he turned pro. When he was playing with the Fighting Saints, he got sent down to the minor leagues in Johnstown, and that was when he first learned to fight.

"I was 19 years old and I played center. The guy who played left wing was 34, and the guy who played right was 28," Holmgren said. "And they were good players in that league. And I was counted on to score, and at that time, there weren't very many of Americans who played pro hockey. It was kind of a new experience, and a lot of people were coming after me, pushing me around and stuff like that. And I remember Coach telling me, 'You better learn to defend yourself pretty quickly here, or you're going to get pushed out of things.' So I had to learn on the job."

Perhaps similar to advice Maurice Richard might have received.

Holmgren's hockey career, however, almost ended before it began when he nearly lost his life while playing for the Richmond Robins, the Flyers AHL affiliate at the time.

Teammate Steve "Coatesy" Coates still shudders when he recalled the event some 30 years later, "We were in Springfield, and there was a bench clear," Coates said. "Homer [Holmgren] was fighting the goalie and who knew how, but he hurt his eye, got a scratched cornea.

"So later that night, we're in Hershey at dinner, and this white liquid is oozing from his eye, and I said, 'We gotta go to the hospital.'"

The team trainer was otherwise occupied at the racetrack, so Coatesy and Homer hailed a taxi to the Hershey hospital, "And there were no cabs in Hershey at the time. We probably found *the one*," Coatesy insists. The doctors examined Holmgren and gave explicit instructions that he not remove the patch from his eye for at least three days. "They were adamant," Coatesy recalls, "positively *adamant*."

The next day Coatesy arrived at practice and as he's lacing up, wondered aloud, "Where's Homer?"

"He got called up last night," a few replied.

Called up?

Yes, to the Flyers, who were playing the Rangers that night, where Holmgren promptly tore off his patch and got ready to test his meddle in the big leagues at Madison Square Garden.

Bobby Clarke remembers, too. After the game in New York,

they headed to Boston, and there was a team meeting. "Homer couldn't hold his head up; it was bad," said Clarke, who—along with Barry Ashbee—took Holmgren to the hospital. "Homer died three times while on the [operating room] table. They brought him back, of course, but it was scary."

Holmgren recovered, of course, and went on to play well for an additional nine NHL seasons despite having compromised eyesight. According to sources, that impediment forced Homer to "skirt a few rules" so he could continue to play in the league, including allegedly memorizing the eye chart because he couldn't see it properly.

In between scraps and fights and penalty box-banishments, Holmgren built a solid career. During his eight seasons in Philadelphia, Holmgren was annually among the team's leaders in penalty minutes and was also able to contribute offense, posting career highs in goals (30) and points (65) in 1979–80, adding an additional 20 points (10 goals and 10 assists) during the Flyers' playoff run.

This is also when he made history: Holmgren's three goals in Game 2 marks the first time a U.S.-born player ever scored a hat trick in a Cup Finals game.

Following an appearance in the 1981 NHL All-Star Game, Holmgren was invited to join the United States' 1981 Canada Cup team[36]. Then just two years later, he was traded to the Minnesota North Stars, leaving Philly with 1,600 penalty minutes, the most in Flyers franchise history up until Rick Tocchet broke the record during the 1991–92 season. He played 27 regular season and 15 playoff games with the North Stars before retiring after the 1984–85 season.

When asked about what he is most proud of during his tenure—whether it's coming back from significant injury or setting such an incredible record, Holmgren states simply, "I'm most proud of the fact that I was just able to play in the National Hockey League at the highest level. I consider it a real honor. It was a very humbling experience for me."

It undoubtedly comes as no shock that Holmgren's greatest memory was playing for the Cup. "That season [1979–80] we had a 35-game unbeaten streak—which is still an NHL record—and we were able to get to the Stanley Cup Finals," he said. "Obviously it was devastating to lose [in overtime of Game 6, the New York Islanders clinched the title, winning their first Cup], but just getting to play for it was tremendous experience, one I'll never forget."

Holmgren recalls his on-ice career fondly, "It went by in the blink of an eye. You think, 'Wouldn't it be nice to turn the clock back and get to do it all over again?' But that only happens in fairytales. There's nothing I would have done differently. It was just a great experience and something I'm proud of."

---

36. Paul Holmgren separated his shoulder at Team USA's Canada Cup training camp in August 1981 and missed the tournament as well as the start of the 1981–82 season.

When asked if he has any funny stories he'd like to share, he chuckles. "Obviously along the way there were some real characters you play with. I remember one thing that started out to be funny, then turned out to be not so funny. We [the Flyers] were in Toronto, and Behn Wilson had bought some gifts for his sister and had them in the back of his [locker room] stall. And [team captain at the time] Mel Bridgman decided to take them and hide them in the locker room, and we all thought it was funny… and Behn did, too…at first. Then he lost his cool, and before we knew it, he had Mel Bridgman around the neck. His feet were dangling; he was actually strangling him right there in the locker room. Mel turned blue," he says. "We had to jump in and save his life."

A father of four, Holmgren's advice to parents is as homespun as it is insightful. "Let your kids have fun," he says. "When I think back to when I was growing up, my dad never said to me after a game, 'You stunk!' or 'You gotta do this better or that better.' After I played he'd just ask me, 'did you have fun out there?'"

And did his mom offer any advice?

"The one thing my mom always said whenever I'd head out to a game was, 'Stay out of the penalty box,'" he laughs, "which obviously I didn't listen to."

———

The year is 1988.

The Winter Olympics are held in Calgary, Alberta, and figure skating is highlighted. These Games see two epic rivalries come toe-to-toe: the "Battle of the Carmens" between Katarina Witt (East Germany) and Debi Thomas (U.S.), and the "Battle of the Brians"[37] between Brian Boitano of the United States and Brian Orser of Canada. Ultimately, in a 5–4 split, the judges awarded Boitano the gold, and Orser the silver. Though Orser wins four judges' votes outright while Boitano wins only three, the two remaining judges that places them with equal total marks gave Boitano a higher technical mark, which was the tiebreaker.[38]

The Games also see an underdog win the hearts of spectators and the media alike: the Jamaican national bobsled team[39] enters its respective competitions with little experience and even

---

37. Brian Orser won the silver medal at the 1984 Winter Olympics while Brian Boitano placed fifth. Orser placed second at the 1985 World Figure Skating Championships and Boitano third. Boitano won the next year. But when Orser won the 1987 Worlds, Boitano knew a change in his skating was imperative if he were to beat Orser at the Calgary Olympics—Orser's home turf. He turned to choreographer Sandra Bezic, who helped change his style of skating. Orser and Boitano were well-matched in many ways: both were excellent skaters who had a jump as their signature move. Going into the Olympics, both were their country's national champions and favorites for the gold.

38. This was the last Olympics in which the technical mark was used as tiebreaker in the long program; in following years the artistic mark was given precedence in the event of tie, which would have changed the split to 6–3 in Orser's favor.

39. The story of the bobsledding team was made into a 1993 Disney comedy film called *Cool Runnings*, directed by Jon Turteltaub.

less of a chance of winning any medals. However, in spite of being outmatched by its competitors, its heart and determination often overshadowed the actual winners, and the unlikely athletes were hailed as heroes for following their dreams despite the odds against them.

It's also the year of the Fog Bowl, when the Eagles are playing the Chicago Bears in the NFC Divisional playoffs, and a dense fog reduces visibility at Soldier Field to 15–20 yards. Despite the fact that the weather inhibited televison and radio announcers from being able to see the field, Eagles quarterback Randall Cunningham had 407 passing yards. Though sidelines or first-down markers are not visible, the Bears ended up winning 20–12.

And in another Philadelphia sport, Paul Holmgren, age 32, had just become the first ever former Flyer to be named as the team's head coach.

Although he started out strong with the Flyers making an unexpected run to the Wales Conference Finals during his first year of coaching, he was fired midway through his fourth season. His subsequent resume includes being a scout, head coach, and interim general manager of the Hartford Whalers.

His front-office career continued with the Flyers in different capacities, including as the Flyers GM.

"More than anything, it's a kids' game," he says. "And we're at the highest level now where it's very much a business, where you have to sell tickets and there's a lot of pressure to win. And we forget that it's supposed to be fun. We lose sight of that. But when you get right down to it, it's still a bunch of grown men playing a kids' game. So I would just tell all the kids out there to have fun. It goes by fast; so just enjoy the game as much as you can."

CHAPTER 7

BRIAN PROPP

A rural farming community in the Canadian province of Saskatchewan, Neudorf is about two square miles and has roughly 300 citizens. Winter lasts eight months of the year, and hockey is the main social outlet in the wintertime, when the farmers aren't as busy.

And it's also where Brian Propp calls home.

————

1964 is a difficult year for Philadelphia on and off the sports field.

During that year the city's infamous race riot, one of the first of such riots of the Civil Rights era, occurs, and 341 people are injured, 774 are arrested, and 225 businesses are damaged.

It is also the year of "The Phold"[40], one of the most notable collapses in sports history. The Phillies finish in a second-place tie in the National League with the Cincinnati Reds (with records of 92–70) just one game behind the NL and World Series-champion St. Louis Cardinals and just two games ahead of the fourth-place San Francisco Giants. Jim Bunning[41] makes history on Father's Day by throwing a perfect game against the New York Mets[42]. But despite the six-and-a-half-game lead with 12 games to play, the Phils go on to lose 10 straight games (the first seven played at home), a devastating free fall that ends in the second-place tie with the Reds.[43]

And Brian Propp is five years old and first learning to skate. Like most kids in his area, after the first snowfall he would

---

40. From 1919 through 1947, the Phillies finished in either last place, or next-to-last place a total of 24 times, inspiring a 1962 cartoon in a baseball magazine depicting a ballplayer arriving at a French Foreign Legion outpost, explaining, "I was released by the Phillies!"

During 1962 and 1963, the Phillies began to climb back to respectability, and throughout the 1964 season, they seemed destined to make it to the World Series with excellent performances from players such as rookie third baseman Dick Allen, Jim Bunning, Chris Short, and star right fielder Johnny Callison. *TV Guide* even went to press with a World Series preview that featured a photo of Connie Mack Stadium.

41. When Jim Bunning retired in 1971 after a 17-year career, he had the second-highest total of career strikeouts in major league history; he is currently 17th. He returned to his native Kentucky and was subsequently elected to the city council, then the state senate before ultimately being elected to the Congress in 1986 (serving in the House from 1987 to 1999) He then became a U.S. Senator, serving as such for 10 years. In July 2009, he announced that he would not run for re-election in 2010. Bunning was inducted into the Baseball Hall of Fame in 1996.

42. The first in the National League since 1880 and the seventh perfect game in Major League Baseball history.

43. The now second-place Phillies traveled to St. Louis to play the Cardinals after their losing homestand and lost the first game—their eighth loss in a row to drop them out of contention. The Cardinals would sweep the three-game set and assume first place for good.

spend hours skating after school on the frozen ponds on the outskirts of town or playing street hockey on the snow-covered roads.

"Growing up and playing out on the ponds was all we knew," Propp says. "Summer was pretty short. We'd play for hours, honing our skating, stickhandling, and shooting skills. At noon-break [lunch] at school, we'd all head out to the pond to play. You'd have to skate through all the grooves, and the bumpy ice would teach you how to stickhandle, and that's why I think so many players from Saskatchewan have been so successful in the NHL over the years."

The neighboring towns were all about 15 or 20 miles apart. So as Propp was growing up, he and his teammates would travel around about a 50-mile radius to play kids in the same age bracket. "There weren't a lot of kids," he said. "So there weren't a lot of teams, and we didn't play a ton of games throughout the year. We'd play against five or six towns, three or four times a year each. Because there weren't that many kids, I used to play on the younger team and the older teams. I was fortunate. I got to play a little bit more. And playing with the older kids helped me to develop a little bit better."

———

Brian Propp began playing Junior B hockey with the Melville Millionaires in 1975 at the age of 16, shattering league records left and right, finishing the season with a staggering 168 points in just 57 games (76 goals and 92 assists).

From there he moved on to the Brandon Wheat Kings, a team that was dominating Canadian major junior hockey at the time, and where he played alongside future Flyers Brad McCrimmon[44] and Ray Allison. "We had a tremendous team," Propp recalled, and he was at the helm, breaking records such as 16 game-winning goals in a single season and accruing a down-right astonishing 511 points in just 213 games over the three years he played with the club (219 goals and 292 assists).

"When I was younger, I didn't follow the NHL that much. We just went out and played and had fun," he says. "It probably

---

44. Hailing from Saskatchewan, Brad McCrimmon was a defenseman who played 18 seasons in the NHL (1979 to 1997). Drafted in the first round (15th overall) by the Boston Bruins in the 1979 Draft, he won the Stanley Cup in 1989 with the Calgary Flames, a team he captained for the 1989–90 season. Throughout his career he was paired with—and helped shape the defensive skills of some of the NHL's best blue liners, including Ray Bourque, Paul Coffey, Chris Pronger, and Mark Howe.

During McCrimmon's tenure with the Flyers (1982–83 to 1986–87), over the course of 367 regular season games played, McCrimmon recorded 187 points (35 goals and 152 assists) and had 355 penalty minutes. During 46 playoff games with the Flyers, he contributed 13 points (7 goals and 6 assists) and 55 penalty minutes. His NHL totals: 1,222 games played, 403 points (81 goals and 322 assists) and 1,416 penalty minutes. And in 116 career playoff games played, he recorded 29 points (11 goals and 18 assists) and 176 penalty minutes.

Following his playing career, he became a coach, spending time with the New York Islanders, the Atlanta Thrashers, the Calgary Flames and, for the last three years of his life, the Detroit Red Wings. He also coached the major junior Saskatoon Blades for two seasons.

wasn't until the second year of junior that I thought there was a possibility I could make the NHL."

———

The year is 1979, a historic and also tragic time in Pennsylvania.

Pope John Paul II makes a much-chronicled visit to Philadelphia, and Three Mile Island, a nuclear plant south of Harrisburg, suffers a core meltdown.

On the ice it is also the year the NHL has what is widely considered the best draft class in history, producing 16 All-Stars

---

On May 19, 2011, it was reported that McCrimmon would leave Detroit to take a head-coaching job in Russia with Lokomotiv Yaroslavl. McCrimmon had been a head coach for only nine preseason games when he died in a plane crash along with all of the Lokomotiv squad before the team's first game of the 2011–12 season, leaving behind wife Maureen, daughter Carlin, and son Liam. Upon learning of McCrimmon's death, Brian Propp said: "Brad McCrimmon was one of my best friends since 1975. We played against each other when he was with the Prince Albert Raiders, and I was with the Melville Millionaires. We played together for three years with the Brandon Wheat Kings and then later with the Flyers. Brad was always the best team leader and always helped all the rookies adjust. I am with Ray Allison now as we are playing a charity hockey and golf event in Canada. We were shocked when we heard the news. Our prayers go out to Brad's family. We are deeply saddened for all the other players and management that were in the crash also. It's a tragic day for hockey."

and five Hall of Famers, including Ray Bourque, Mark Messier, Glenn Anderson, and Michel Goulet.

Brian Propp remembers coming in from a long, back-breaking day working on the farm and getting the phone call that would change his life. "At that time we weren't all shuttled into the draft," he says. "I came home that night and got a call from Pat Quinn and Keith Allen, telling me that I'd just been drafted by the Philadelphia Flyers. We didn't really pay that much attention to it at the time. I mean, I was a little disappointed I wasn't picked earlier in the draft, but I also knew I was going to a really good team and felt I fit into the Flyers style of play. And I was really excited about that."

Propp started his career off in a spectacular fashion: his first NHL goal was a game-winner in his first career game, playing alongside veterans Reggie Leach and Bobby Clarke.

It was a sign of good things to come, as Propp's NHL statistics are nothing short of remarkable. In 1,016 regular season games played, he amassed 1,004 points (425 goals and 579 assists); in 160 playoff games, he had 148 points (64 goals and 84 assists).

A particularly fond memory of his career was playing on the line with Wayne Gretzky and Mario Lemieux for the Canada Cup. "It was sort of thing people dream about," Propp says. "The hockey at that level was just incredible. Especially in '87 when we'd [the Flyers] just lost [the Stanley Cup] to the Oilers that summer. After losing in seven games, to come back and be on the winning side was pretty special."

Propp attributes much of his success to following the advice of his dad, who told him to "concentrate on the fundamentals [of] skating, shooting, being accurate with your shot, hitting the net, always working on getting a little better strength-wise, on getting quicker and also the mental part of the game—trying to think where the puck is going to be, rather than just react to it, being pro-active."

Propp has the enviable distinction of making it to the Stanley Cup Finals five times during the career as well as the unenviable distinction of never having won a Cup. "It's tougher now," he says. "Looking back at it, a couple of bounces either way, and I could've had two or three Cups. But it's not just about winning the Cup; it's about giving 100 percent of your effort and trying your best. And I look at it as helping the team to get a chance just to be there. And looking at the teams we lost to, some of them were the most powerful teams in hockey.

"It's disappointing, but a lot of players never even get that far. Having won the Canada Cup and the Spangler Cup for Team Canada [in 1992], at least being on the winning side a couple of times makes things a little easier."

When asked for advice, Propp says: "Give 100 percent and be happy with your effort. That's what my dad taught me."

And if anyone should be proud of his efforts, it's Brian Propp. In 1994, he ended his exemplary 15-year career on a high note. During his last NHL season, he played both his 1,000th NHL game and scored his 1,000th NHL point.

When he thinks back to when he first arrived in Philly from the farm in Saskatchewan, he just remembers one thing. "I was in awe," he says. "I was a little naïve, but thankfully there was a lot of leadership guys like Frank Bathe and Bobby Clarke and Bob Kelly who helped show me around and just took care of me. It was a big adjustment for a couple of years just to even get used to finding your way around."

But Propp has called the Delaware Valley home ever since. A true Philadelphia Flyer to the core, he ranks second in Flyers franchise history in goals (369, which is behind Bill Barber), second in assists (480 and behind Clarke), and third in overall games played (behind both Clarke and Barber).

And to think it all began on the frozen ponds skirting a small farming village called Neudorf, a town of only 300 people and nearly 2,000 miles away from America's birthplace.

CHAPTER 8

TIM KERR

He holds the NHL record for most power play goals in a single season (34) as well as the Flyers franchise record for the most 50-goal seasons (four). He shares the NHL playoff record for most goals in a period (four) and the most points in a period (four). During his playoff appearances (81 games), he had 71 points (40 goals and 31 assists) and 58 penalty minutes. He made three All-Star appearances and was awarded the Bill Masterton Memorial Trophy in 1989.

In one game alone, Game 3 of the 1985 Patrick Division semifinals against the Rangers, Kerr set or tied four NHL records that he still holds today, including fastest four goals in a playoff game (8:16) and most power play goals in a period (three).

All of which is wholly impressive by anyone's standards. So it's shocking that Tim Kerr didn't start playing hockey until he was nine, which, "is late particularly for a Canadian kid," he says.

What's even more surprising is that he never played travel hockey and was—by his own admission—"incredibly uncoordinated" for most of his young life. He also was not drafted.

But it's true.

———

The year is 1969.

Major League Baseball celebrates the 100th anniversary of professional baseball, and the NFL celebrates its 50th regular season.

It's also the year of two incredible upsets: the upstart "Miracle Mets" beat the favored Orioles in five games, becoming the first expansion team to win a World Series, while the formidable Lakers led by Elgin Baylor, Wilt Chamberlain, and Jerry West were beat in the finals by the Celtics—an aging team that barely made the playoffs, yet went on to make history as the first road team ever to win Game 7 of the NBA Finals.

And Tim Kerr is learning to play hockey in his hometown of Tecumseh, a community near Windsor in southeastern Ontario, made up of about 5,000 residents at the time.

"I guess I was like most Canadians," he says. "My dad built a rink in the backyard. And if we didn't have ice in the rink, we were playing street hockey in the parking lot at the school across the street or on Lake Erie and the Detroit River when they would freeze up.

"Like most kids all we did was play hockey. One of the great things that I look back on—especially now as a father—is how dedicated my dad was. We had a double rink in town, and of course, there was never any ice time for us little guys. The only ice time was in the middle of the night. And my dad worked real hard. He had two jobs, but he would get up at one in the morning and drive me to the rink. And then come home, go back to bed, and come back and get me at 4 or 4:30 AM. He never said, 'no', never even questioned it. He was a phenomenal father. And I look back at that as something that really helped in terms of me getting that extra time to get better."

During Kerr's time spent playing junior hockey, he was known as a slow skater who spent a lot of time in front of the net. He was viewed as a decent scorer but not especially remarkable. However, after a 40-goal season, his whole life changed during a transcendent year for Philadelphia sports.

During 1980 the Phillies' Tug McGraw strikes out Willie Wilson, ending 97 years of frustration by defeating the American League champion Kansas City Royals for the Phillies' first-ever World Championship. Quarterback Ron "Jaws" Jaworski[45] also leads the Eagles through an exemplary regular season (12–4). The Eagles win the NFC East for the first time. They defeat the Minnesota Vikings in the divisional round of the playoffs and the Dallas Cowboys in the NFC championship game to reach the franchise's first ever Super Bowl. The 76ers lose to the Los Angeles Lakers due in part to the electrifying play of rookie Magic Johnson, who takes over playing center for the Lakers

---

45. That same year Jaworski was named the UPI NFL Player of the Year and he also received the Bert Bell Award, the Maxwell Football Club's Professional Player of the Year award, and the Professional Athlete of the Year award.

in place of Kareem Abdul-Jabbar[46], in Game 6 and scores 42 points.

And Tim Kerr, then 20, is about to begin his first season as a member of the Philadelphia Flyers organization.

Right away he suited up with the Maine Mariners (the Flyers' AHL affiliate at the time) and scored six points in seven games. Although he made a fairly good showing at the Flyers' training camp, he had not convinced everyone that he was NHL material. Luck, however, was on his side when a spot opened on the roster due to another player's broken leg.

Kerr recorded more than 20 goals during his first two seasons, and by his third, he was on track to surpass the 40-goal mark when a serious knee injury ended his season.

Always a late bloomer, Kerr says that, as he grew older and became more comfortable in his 6'3", 230-pound frame, things began to come together for him. But the real turning point, he said, was when he came to Philly: "I learned what conditioning was, more than I'd ever really been taught before, and I think that's what got me over the hump. When I worked out with Pat Croce rehabbing my knee, that's what helped get me to the next level strength-wise."

The following season Kerr and teammates Brian Propp and Dave Poulin emerged as one of the most dangerous offensive

---

46. Kareem Abdul-Jabbar was sidelined because of a sprained ankle sustained in Game 5 of the Series.

lines in the NHL, and Kerr recorded his first of four consecutive 50-goal seasons. Not since Phil Esposito, had the NHL seen a player dominate the slot as well as Kerr, earning him the nickname "the Sultan of Slot."

As it became apparent that Kerr's mere presence on the ice could change the momentum of any given game, he became one of the most feared and diligently checked forwards in the league. He astounded spectators and opponents alike with his ability to withstand physical abuse while using his superior hand-eye coordination to score night after night for years.

During both the 1985–86 and 1986–87 seasons, he recorded 58 goals and led the Flyers to the Finals against the Edmonton Oilers twice in three years. In 1987, however, Kerr suffered a devastating shoulder injury and was not able to play in the Finals, and his presence was sorely missed. The Flyers were defeated, which prompted many to believe that—as solid as a team the Flyers had—they just could not do it without Kerr.

———

His NHL career spanned 13 years, totaling 655 games played within which he accrued an amazing 674 points (370 goals and 304 assists) and 596 penalty minutes.

Overcoming his size and physical awkwardness as a child, however, wasn't the only adversity he faced.

Kerr's career was plagued with injuries, including hospitalization with aseptic meningitis and five shoulder operations in a mere 14-month period, causing him to miss almost the complete 1982–83 and 1987–88 seasons. He also endured the tragic death of his wife, Kathy at age 30, just 10 days after the birth of their baby.

But Kerr's outlook remains positive.

"I think I was very fortunate to play with the Flyers organization. Injuries were obviously tough, but I don't think I would change anything," he says. "We had great success. We went to the Finals twice. If I thought I was playing with a team that didn't put it all out there, then you might look back and have some regrets. But that wasn't the case. We had guys that played hurt, giving everything they had night after night. We just came up short. I don't look back at the negatives because I had such a great time."

And despite all that he had to overcome, Kerr was a powerhouse during his prime, prompting Hockey Hall of Famer Bryan Trottier to once joke that the only way to stop Kerr was to wrap chains around his arms and legs. He then retracted that statement almost immediately and quipped, "But that still probably wouldn't stop him."

"When I look back, there's a few things I'm most proud of," Kerr says. "When I think of the great teams we had in the mid-'80s where we had a great group of guys who were all there for the right reasons, where guys played hurt, where pretty much on any given night we felt as a team we had a chance of winning that game…It was a great time. The other thing is when the Flyers inducted me into their Hall of Fame the year after I retired, which was probably the biggest honor I've had in my career."

But Kerr's fond memories aren't confined to his time on the ice; he remembers some funny stories from off the ice as well.

"When Dave Brown came up from Portland [The Flyers' affiliate at the time]—and someone, I think Davey Poulin—had told him that when he was driving and he came up to a toll-booth, he didn't have to pay. He just had to yell into the basket that he played for the Flyers. He believed it for a while, and we all had a good laugh at that one," he says. "Another time, Rick MacLeish or Billy Barber put some hot stuff on Pat Croce's workout gear, and it started to burn as soon as he put his clothes on. He wasn't too happy, but it sure was funny."

These days, though, Kerr spends his time running his successful South Jersey shore real estate agency and enjoys ownership of the Pensacola Ice Flyers and part-ownership of the Mississippi Surge, teams of the Southern Professional Hockey League.

But his top priorities are his wife, two daughters, and three sons.

"Now, as a dad, I never miss any of my kids' events," Kerr says. "I go and watch and just enjoy them. And that's something really important that I learned from my dad. Although he was never much for advice, he never missed a game; he was just always there and was always a fan of me and my brother. He just enjoyed watching us play.

"As a parent I've tried to learn from my upbringing—and I wouldn't say that I'm perfect at it, but I certainly try to let my kids find their way. For me it's just about being there and supporting them, win or lose. I'm lucky. I've always had a great relationship with my kids, and I'm able to talk to them after a game about what went well, what didn't go so well. So that they know I'm a positive influence, but at the same time I'm willing to tell them what I think the negatives were, but not in an emotional way, which I think my kids respect. And they know that I'm certainly their biggest fan."

Kerr's advice for young, aspiring athletes is simple and heartfelt: "Do what you love to do," he says. "Work hard and stay out of trouble. And if you stay positive, good things will happen. Have that dream and never give up on that dream, because they do come true. I never gave up and I'd like to have a dollar for every person that said I'd never be a hockey player."

And when you take a look at Kerr's inspirational career—one that defied so many odds and was so fun to watch—we should all be grateful he did not listen to the naysayers.

CHAPTER 9

BRAD MARSH

In the Philadelphia sports area, 1962 stands as a significant year.

The Phillies celebrate their 80th season as a franchise, finishing the season in seventh place in the National League with a record of 81–80 (a dramatic improvement compared to their 47–107 of the previous season). During March they retire Robin Roberts' No. 36 jersey when the Yankees visit Clearwater for a spring training game. (The Phillies sold Roberts to the Yankees shortly after the previous season).[47]

Philly native and Overbrook High School alum Wilt Chamberlain has perhaps the most dominate season in NBA history. He averages a league-leading and NBA record 50.4 points. During an eight day stretch in January, he records three games where he scores at least 62 points. Nothing, however, was quite as spectacular as the March 2 game against the New York Knicks when Chamberlain has the most epic game in

---

47. This was the first uniform number to be retired by the Phillies organization and only the second time (after the Yankees retired Babe Ruth's number 3) that a uniform number was retired while the player was still active. Robin Roberts started for the Yankees in the spring game, gave up four runs in three innings, and was the winning pitcher as he carried the Yankees to victory, 13–10.

NBA history, scoring 100 points before 4,124 fans in Hershey, Pennsylvania.[48]

And Brad Marsh, age four, has just received his first pair of skates from Santa Claus.

"I had two brothers, so hockey was very big in our household. Whether it was playing hockey on the outdoor rink on our front yard with a fire hydrant right in the middle of it or on the corner pond, you played hockey morning, noon, and night. And when there was no ice, you played road hockey morning, noon, and night. We also played down in the basement all the time. So it was hockey 12 months a year.

"There was no satellite or cable TV. So we had hockey on Wednesday nights and Saturday nights, and the Wednesday night game was always 'joined in progress,' if you can imagine that," he says. "And then Saturday night we got to stay up a little bit later than usual to watch the game. It was always a big deal, and we always got a treat—snacks that we all take for granted today....They weren't around much when we were growing up. So every Saturday night it was *Hockey Night in Canada*, with three boys sitting on the sofa sharing

---

48. Despite his dominance Wilt Chamberlain would lose out to Bill Russell for the coveted title of NBA MVP just as the Warriors finished second behind Russell's Boston Celtics with a 49–31 record, setting the stage for a battle between the two greats in the Eastern Division Finals. The pair would battle neck and neck for seven games, as the final game was tied 107–107 in the final seconds. However, it would be Sam Jones—not Russell—sinking the winning shot with just two seconds remaining, breaking the hearts of Philadelphia sports fans.

a bowl of popcorn or some potato chips....Man, you were in heaven.

"Back then most communities were the same. We were pretty a much a one-sport town [in London, Ontario], and a one-sport family. The option of soccer was not there like it is now; the option of baseball was not there. Down in the States, the kids played baseball, football, basketball...where in Canada we were pretty much a one-sport country especially back in the early '60s when I grew up. Everybody played hockey.... There were only two teams in Canada, of course: Montreal and Toronto. But London has close proximity to Detroit. So in our area, you cheered for one of those three teams. In the Marsh household, we were Maple Leafs fans. And when you played road hockey you played every position, and you were always someone on the Leafs. Sometimes you were Johnny Bower making the big save, sometimes you were Tim Horton, Allan Stanley, and so on, and so on. You were always one of your idols during those hockey games, and many times it was in the pre-tense: 'Here we are in Game 7 of the Stanley Cup Finals' and you go down and you shoot and you score. We imitated all the players we saw on TV.

"I didn't play any organized hockey till I was seven years old. When I grew up, you just played for the community that you lived in, and London was divided up into various geographical areas. I played for the Southwest London Bobcats, and every-thing was basically a house league. And then they developed a competitive team, but it was just more or less an extension of what we did on the pond. It was just a little more organized— organized into age groups. I was pretty fortunate. Once we got on the competitive team, I had the same coach for four or five years. His name was Bruce Stewart. In modern minor hockey, most associations prohibit coaches from coaching the same team more than two years in a row because of favoritism and all that stuff. So I was pretty lucky to have the same coach growing up and I was pretty lucky to have Bruce Stewart. And what I remember from him was that he instilled in me and my teammates that hockey was all about hard work and doing your best and nothing else mattered. We were expected to perform at the highest level we could, and laziness was not tolerated or accepted, and that just stayed with me: that work ethic stayed with me my whole career—through minor, junior, all the way to pro."

Excellent at reading plays and known for using his angles with finesse, it's hard to picture Marsh as playing anything but defense, and his first coach realized it, too. "When I first started, I played center," Marsh says. "But my coach put me back on the blue line because I was the biggest kid.

"My last two years of junior, when I was 18, 19…people started talking, saying 'He does have a chance to play pro,' whereas before my mind-set was just to play hockey the best I could. I was lucky enough to make the jump from the Southwest London Bobcats to play Junior B and then to play Junior A, where some of my friends weren't so fortunate and I just enjoyed playing the game and didn't think of where it was taking me. I just wanted to play hockey."

———

The year is 1978.

The great-great-grandson of Triple Crown winners War Admiral and Man o' War, Affirmed becomes the 11th and most recent winner of the Triple Crown, while a single off Expos pitcher Steve Rogers makes Pete Rose the 13th player in major league history to collect 3,000 career hits and launches his run at Joe DiMaggio's record 56-game hitting streak, which had stood virtually unchallenged for 37 years.

And Brad Marsh, age 20, is drafted by the Atlanta Flames (now relocated to Calgary) 11th overall, ahead of names such as Al Secord, Larry Playfair, Tony McKegney, and Stan Smyl.

"The draft nowadays is a huge production, but when you talk to guys from my era, they didn't go to the draft," he says. "They were home working on the family farm or wherever, and they found out about it that night or the next day. It was one of the first years where some players went to the draft, and I was one of them. At the time my agent was Alan Eagleson, and he took a number of his clients that were projected to go high in the draft down, including me. So we took a bus from Toronto to Montreal. And my parents came from London, and we just sat in the back of the hotel ballroom and waited for my name to be called. And it was called—11th overall, the first round and it was quite a neat feeling. You were able to share that moment with just your parents as opposed to nowadays with all the cameras and media people around.

"I was drafted to Atlanta, and when you get drafted in the NHL, it's a huge thrill…but it was somewhat of a head-scratcher because I really didn't know where Atlanta was. I knew it was in the States obviously and I knew it was in Georgia, but I had never been there, never cheered for them, never really seen them on TV. And all of a sudden—I'm drafted by them and going to be playing for them…so it was a little bit of a let-down if you will—that I didn't get drafted by one of the Original Six teams. But that goes away pretty soon, once you start playing."

Marsh made the jump immediately into the NHL.

"And then we were all sold to Calgary—the whole franchise—and then, while in Calgary, I was named captain, and at the time I was the youngest captain in the NHL," he says. "And the reason I bring that up is because when you're captain of the team, you think everything's going pretty good and you think you got the world by the proverbial tail if you will…and then I got traded to Philadelphia, and whenever it comes up I always say, 'I played in the NHL, and I was a pretty good defenseman, and I was captain of the team, and I thought I was doing everything I was supposed to be doing.' I still got traded."

Marsh's debut in the league included playing in 257 consecutive games with the Flames of which the last 97 came as team captain. During those four seasons, the solid defenseman and team leader recorded 44 points and 317 penalty minutes and six points and 27 penalty minutes during 22 playoff games.

———

Brad Marsh, age 23, arrived in Philly in November 1981 ready to lace up and play with his new club.

"It wasn't until my trade to Philadelphia that I learned what it took to be a professional athlete. There was more to the game than just playing the game. I was still just playing the game in the NHL as I did as a kid: happy to be there, worked hard, played hard but also enjoyed the life of being an NHL player...and when I got traded to Philadelphia it was the first time that I got extra training. It was the first time I'd ever lifted weights. It was the first time there was a strength and conditioning coach [Pat Croce], and it was really the first time I walked in the dressing room, and there was leadership there that held you accountable. Pat Quinn was the coach, and I've got all the time in the world for Pat. But from a player standpoint, there was also your dad [Bobby Clarke], and Paul Holmgren, and so on, and so on. And so it was just a huge eye-opener for me, even though I'd been captain of the Flames, and then all of a sudden, things weren't going real well for me in Philadelphia because I thought I was just good enough to play hockey. But it was there that I learned there's a lot more that goes into being a professional hockey player than just that. Getting traded to Philly was the best thing that happened to me. I ended up playing 15 years, and that would not have happened had I not played in Philadelphia. Just the organization—from top down—it's all about winning and all about creating a professional. It's all: 'This is how we go about it in Philadelphia.'"

"Brad was a very important leader on our team. Marshy was all about the team and never for himself," former teammate Mark Howe told Greatest Hockey Legends.com. "He could play 20-plus minutes a game and could always be counted on to compete each and every night. He was a great shot blocker and a rugged competitor on the ice but a gentle and kind person off the ice. Brad was always smiling and loved to be at the rink each and every day. For many years he was a mainstay on the blue line for our team and a big reason why the Flyers had a successful and competitive team in the '80s."

"Marshy came to play every single night," teammate Dave Poulin told the website. "What was understated was his leadership role both on and off the ice. He was an enormous positive factor in many young players' careers."

Marsh loved playing in Philadelphia.

"The Philadelphia sports scene is second to none in North America," he says. "It's just phenomenal, and this year's Winter Classic was just the icing on the cake with the fan support that was there for three games. People in the hockey world—especially in Canada—don't seem to realize how loyal and die-hard the Philly fans are. The Flyers are the only team they cheer for and the only team they care about, and they hate everybody else…whereas you go to a lot of other communities—especially in Canada—when Ottawa and Toronto play here in Ottawa, half the arena is cheering for Toronto, and that's at our home game. And that's because there are so many Toronto fans throughout Canada, and it's the same when Calgary comes here, and so on. In Canada they cheer for a superstar player that might play for another team, but Philadelphia is different; it's the only hockey they've ever known. So they live and breathe Flyers wins and losses, and Mr. [Ed] Snider was the first one to introduce cable TV. So even when you couldn't attend a Flyers game, you could sit home and cheer for them on TV, which back in the '60s and '70s was unheard of. The Flyer fans are very passionate, very knowledgeable about the game. And what they want to see is hard work; they don't want to see a prima donna out there, loafing through a hockey game, because they'll let him know it, and as well they should.

"The Flyers have been such a successful organization and yes, there's tension and pressure to win each and every game, but it is such a great organization that you are relaxed when you're a Flyer. Now that might sound a little corny because as I said there's enormous pressure on you to win, but it is such a great environment that it's easy to be yourself. It's easy to play a prank or a practical joke and so on, where there's other teams—and even other offices—that when there's tension and you're worried about this or that or you don't like the boss, you don't like the owner, nobody has any fun—period—whether it's a dressing room or an office. Whereas with the Flyers, Mr. Snider has created such an atmosphere that it's easy to be comfortable, and it's easy to have a solid team base."

Despite the fact that Marsh played a lot of junior hockey and was drafted in the first round, things were not always smooth sailing. "Things seemed to be okay. I started in the '70s, but then through the '80s with the high-flying Oilers, the game seemed to be changing a little bit to speed, speed, speed. Everybody had to be fast, and everyone had to be nimble and agile with good stickhandling. I joke about it now—I played fifteen years, over a thousand games in the league and I couldn't shoot, skate, or stickhandle," he says. "My NHL career—especially the last half of it—I sat out or was traded or moved… always because they said I was too slow. I was not a graceful skater, and when people used to say, 'Brad Marsh is too slow to play in today's NHL,' or 'Marsh can't play four-on-four; there's too much open ice'….That used to just drive me crazy and made me work harder. And maybe I wasn't a beautiful skater, but I got the job done. And I've always said, 'When I got from A to B, I knew what to do when I got to B,' where there are so many players who are beautiful skaters who don't have a clue as to how to play the game. I had to prove myself year after year after year that I could play with the best of them."

Marsh's response was to work hard both on and off the ice to improve his strength and quickness…not his gracefulness.

"You can do it ugly," he says. "You don't have to become a beautiful skater."

Whether it was minor hockey, junior hockey, or the NHL, Marsh was either the captain or the assistant captain of every single team he played on.

"I liked being one of the go-to guys, and it goes back to Bruce Stewart and some of the other coaches I've had along the way that instilled in me the importance of work ethic," Marsh says. "Leaders come in all shapes and sizes; there are fire-and-brimstone guys, and then there are guys that just lead by example. And with the exception of this year, I've coached every year since I retired, and that ranges from the lowest rung of house league to the top level of competitive hockey to boys, girls, AAA, to juniors. I've coached everywhere, and my simple advice to parents would be: be quiet and enjoy it. It's something these kids are going to remember for the rest of their lives, and it's over before you know it, and so many parents get wrapped up in the moment. 'Oh my son only got 10 minutes of ice time today.' Well, instead of blaming everybody and making a fuss, forget it. He might get 15 the next game. It always evens out at the end of the day. So just sit back and enjoy it. And for their kids, don't let a coach pigeonhole you by saying, 'You're a defensive defenseman, or you're a power forward, or whatever'—the main thing is as a kid you have to keep improving and keep working on your game. And there are far too many young kids who are becoming specialists at a particular part of the game, and I'd love to see kids play all the positions, move around, and play the game. And my advice is the same to kids as it is to parents—enjoy the environment that you're in. Work your butt off, and you'll enjoy it that much more."

So in his fifteen years in the NHL, what is Marsh most proud of?

"I'm proud of a lot of things," he says. "I played a long time in the NHL and I was a part of some really good hockey teams, and I look back and I don't have a bad word to say about anything that I experienced over my hockey career. You know, I was traded, I was released, I was benched. You name it, I tasted it all. But looking back, I don't have a negative thing to say about any of it because in the end it just made me stronger."

CHAPTER 10

MARK HOWE

It's midsummer of 2011.

Michael Nutter is the mayor of Philadelphia, which is currently enduring its sixth heat wave of the season, and the Phillies have what many believe is the greatest pitching rotation of all time. The NFL lockout is now over, and it has just been announced that Flyers chairman Ed Snider will be inducted into the U.S. Hockey Hall of Fame in the fall.

And Mark Howe also has just learned he will be inducted into the Hockey Hall of Fame.

"It was a nice surprise. I didn't think it was going to happen," Howe says. "Getting that phone call was pretty exciting."

It's hard to believe a player of Howe's caliber was surprised. After all, Howe—a three-time runner up for the Norris Trophy[49]—made the Stanley Cup finals three times during his solid 16 years in the NHL and had four All-Star appearances.

But let's go back to when it all began.

The year is 1959.

---

49. Given by the Professional Hockey Writers' Association to the League's Best Defenseman.

FLYER LIVES

Alaska and Hawaii are admitted as the 49th and 50th states, and a plane crashes in Iowa, killing musicians Buddy Holly, Ritchie Valens, Roger Peterson, and the Big Bopper. It is also the year the Barbie doll debuts.

The Baltimore Colts win 31–16 against the New York Giants to become that year's NFL champs, and in August the American Football League[50] is founded.

There are only six teams in the NHL, and Mark Howe is just four years old, embarking on his first year of organized hockey, where there is not one indoor rink in the entire city of Detroit aside from where the Red Wings play.

---

50. The AFL was a major American Professional Football league that operated from 1960 until 1969 when it then merged with the National Football League.

51. Generally regarded as one of the greatest hockey players of all time, Gordie Howe is most famous for his scoring prowess, physical strength, and career longevity, and was the recipient of the first NHL Lifetime Achievement Award (2008).

Referred to as Power, Mr. Everything, Mr. All-Star, the Most, the Great Gordie, the King of Hockey, the Legend, the Man, No. 9, and "Mr. Elbows" (for his tough physical play), he is perhaps best known by the moniker that says it all: "Mr. Hockey."

A 23-time NHL All-Star (a league record), four-time Stanley Cup champion, winner of both the Art Ross Memorial Trophy and Hart Memorial Trophy six times each, Gordie Howe was among the top five in NHL scoring for 20 consecutive seasons.

He holds the NHL records for the most NHL games played (1,767), the most consecutive NHL 20-goal seasons (22), the most games played for a single franchise (1,687, Detroit), the most goals and points with a single franchise (786 and 1,809, respectively, Detroit), the most NHL and WHA regular season games played (2,186), the most NHL and WHA regular season and playoff games played (2,421), the most NHL seasons played (26), the most NHL and WHA

"If it was snowing, we used to get two players from each team because there were only four shovels, and you'd have to take a break every 10 minutes to shovel the rink," Howe recalls. "Then, over the course of that winter, Mom and Dad got a few people together and got the use of an old broken-down factory, and the next year someone put boards underneath the building. It was still all-natural ice, but at least we didn't have to deal with the snow."

Howe and his brother, Marty, used to play with neighborhood kids on a rink his parents put up in the front yard. "The only problem was we couldn't play at night," Mark Howe says. "So what we started doing was instead of decorating the house

---

seasons played (32), the most NHL regular season goals by a right winger (801), the most NHL regular season assists by a right winger (1,049), the most NHL regular season points by a right winger (1,850), the most times leading NHL playoffs in scoring (six times), and the most NHL regular season points by a father/son combo (2,592), with son, Mark.

Gordie Howe was the first player to score over 1,000 goals (WHA and NHL, regular season and playoff combined), and the first player to reach 1,500 games played in NHL history.

At age 52, Howe was the oldest NHL player at the time of retirement, the oldest player to play in an NHL game, the only player to ever play in the NHL after age 50, and the only player to play in the NHL in five different decades (1940s, 1950s, 1960s, 1970s, and 1980s)

In 1998, *The Hockey News* released its list of top 100 NHL Players of All Time and listed Howe third overall (ahead of Mario Lemieux but behind Wayne Gretzky and Bobby Orr). Upon learning of the rankings, Orr was quoted as regarding Howe as the greatest player.

A 12-foot-tall statue weighing about 4,500 pounds was erected in his honor at Joe Louis Arena, while another was erected in downtown Saskatoon, Saskatchewan, where Howe is depicted wearing a Red Wings sweater. (The statue has since been relocated to the Credit Union Centre.)

for Christmas, we decorated the rink with Christmas lights so we could play night hockey."

Howe remembers missing one night that shattered the big picture window in the front of his house. "It was around 9 PM. Dad was out of town, so we had to board it up and wait until the next day when the man from the hardware store could come over to fix it. It was the dead of winter, of course," he chuckles. "So that didn't go over too well with Mom."

"Dad" of course, is Gordie Howe, aka "Mr. Hockey," one of the greatest players to have ever graced the ice.[51] Having an iconic superstar hockey player for a father has some drawbacks, of course, including being constantly compared and being the first one to be picked on by the opposition, but Howe remembers the advice of his mom: "She told me to always set *my own* goals."

But having Gordie Howe for a Dad certainly had its perks, too. "When the old Olympia [Stadium] was changing nets, or the guys [Red Wings] were getting rid of equipment, we [he and brother Marty] used to go down and get it before they threw it away," he said. "So our hockey games in the yard were probably as good as anyone could have because we had all NHL authentic stuff. It was neat."

Another advantage was having his very own locker in the Red Wings locker room at the age of 12 and getting to go to practice and scrimmage against the team.

———

One of the most memorable experiences of Howe's early career came at age 16.

The year is 1972.

Gasoline was 36 cents a gallon, and a postage stamp cost eight cents.

U.S. president Richard Nixon orders the development of the space shuttle program and announces that no new draftees will be sent to Vietnam before finding himself at the center of one of the worst political disgraces in history—the Watergate scandal—which two years later would lead to the only resignation of a U.S. president in history.

In hockey news, it's the 56th season of the National Hockey League with all 16 teams playing 78 games each, including two new teams—the New York Islanders and the Atlanta Flames. For the third consecutive season, the Chicago Black Hawks dominate the West Division while the Montreal Canadiens take over first place in the East Division—and the league—from the Boston Bruins, ultimately winning the Cup by beating Chicago 4–2. No teams in the playoffs sweep their opponents, the last time this would happen until 1991.

It's also the inaugural season of the World Hockey Association, which signed several top players, including Bobby Hull and Derek Sanderson and it's the year Paul Henderson[52] scores "the Goal of the Century" for Team Canada to win the

Summit Series[53], the first ever hockey showdown between Canada and the Soviet Union.

And at age 16, Mark Howe becomes the youngest hockey player to ever win an Olympic medal.

"It was kind of a fluke. I had hurt my knee the year before," he says. "And they thought it was just a ligament that was going to heal, and it turned out to be cartilage, but they didn't find out until the fall. So I had to have surgery. If I hadn't, I probably would've been up in Toronto playing junior hockey. My first exhibition game [after the surgery] was against the Olympic team, and about two weeks later, a guy got hurt so they asked me to come try out for a spot. It wasn't in the plans. It just ended up working out great. I missed two, two and half months of school…but the learning experience was just incredible."

Another remarkable experience for Howe came the following year when he decided to play in the World Hockey Association (WHA) with his brother, Marty, and his father, Gordie.

---

52. A left-winger, Paul Henderson played 13 NHL seasons for the Detroit Red Wings, Toronto Maple Leafs and Atlanta Flames.

53. Prior to the start of the season, the 1972 Summit Series took place, the first ever meeting between Soviet Union and NHL caliber Canadian hockey players, a match Canada was expected win handily. But as the games began, Team Canada was shocked to find itself with a losing record of one win, two losses, and a tie after four games in Canada. In Game 4, which Canada lost 5–3, Vancouver fans echoed the rest of Canada's sentiments by booing them off the ice. The final four games were played in the Soviet Union. Canada lost Game 5, but won the last three for a final record of four wins, three losses, and a tie.

———

The year is 1973.

O.J. Simpson becomes the first player in NFL history to rush for more than 2,000 yards in a single season, and the Miami Dolphins win Super Bowl VII to complete the only perfect[54] season in the modern NFL era.

It's when George Foreman beats Joe Frazier by a knockout in two rounds to lift the world's heavyweight champion title from Frazier, and when famed "Battle of the Sexes" takes place at Houston's Astrodome when tennis legend Billie Jean King defeats Bobby Riggs in three straight sets.

And Gordie Howe "Mr. Hockey" comes out of retirement to play with his sons in what is one of the most remarkable comebacks in sports history.

Still a left-winger, Mark Howe recalls the experience fondly. "It was pretty cool. I consider my dad the best hockey player ever," he says. "And we just had awesome chemistry together on the ice. You didn't have to look; you didn't have to talk. You knew what the other guy was going to do two seconds before he did it. So for me, that made it extra special."

At age 45 Gordie Howe had been retired for two years when he came to training camp in Houston. "Marty and I went home to Mom and said, 'We don't think he can make it.' He was really

---

54. Unbeaten and untied.

having a rough time for about a month or so. But within six weeks, we couldn't keep up with him," Mark Howe says. "His endurance, his stamina, and strength at 45 was just absolutely phenomenal."

Gordie Howe went on to win MVP of the league that year, and son—and Philly favorite—Mark earned the Lou Kaplan Rookie of the Year Award.

After four years with Houston, the Howe trio played for what was then called the New England Whalers before the WHA ultimately folded. When the remaining teams of the defunct WHA merged with the NHL, the WHA teams were allowed to keep only two players while the rest were placed in a league-wide draft. Mark Howe was one of the players the Whalers chose to keep.

Although this solidified Howe's value to the team, it also marked a change in Howe's play. Still primarily a winger, he was playing more and more on the blue line, and it led to a position change that would allow him to blossom as one of the most solid, intelligent defensemen in the NHL.

This move to defense came as no surprise to at least one person whom Howe recalls getting some particularly unforgettable advice from when he was about 15. Howe was playing in a tier-two league in Detroit, and at the end of practice one day, "Coach [Carl Lindstrom] skates by and said, 'You're going to be in the NHL some day. And you're going to be a great defenseman.' I looked at him like I thought there was something wrong with him," Howe laughs. "He was a very patient man, a great teacher who not only taught us a lot of things on the ice, but off the ice as well. His foresight back then was pretty awesome because I was a winger, leading the league in scoring by about 10, 15 points as a 15-year-old kid when everybody else was 18, 19. And he's telling me I'm going to be a great defenseman. I thought he was half-goofy."

But clearly Lindstrom was onto something. Howe is widely regarded as one of the best two-way defensemen of the 1980s, the decade he played with the Flyers.

But Howe's time with the Whalers wasn't always a bed of roses. In fact, while playing with them, Howe suffered one of the worst injuries in hockey history, prompting the NHL to reconfigure the structure of the nets.

———

The year is 1980, a miraculous year in hockey when the U.S. Olympic Team defeats the Soviet team—widely considered to be the best hockey team in the world at the time—to go on to the next round to beat Finland for the gold[55], prompting *Sports Illustrated* to call it "the Top Sports Moment of the 20th Century."

And Mark Howe, then 25 years old, loses his balance as he's chasing a loose puck in his own zone and goes feet-first

---

55. The Soviet Union took the silver medal by beating Sweden in its final game.

into the goal, sliding into the pointed metal center of the net, essentially impaling him. The five-inch gash in his upper thigh and buttock nearly ends his career, but what is most terrifying about the incident is that the metal just misses his spinal column. To prevent other players from such a fate as Howe's, the NHL installs safer nets that no longer had a center portion that juts up toward the goal line and has magnetic fasteners that allow the goal to become dislodged more easily. He lost 35 pounds due to the liquid diet he is placed on to avoid intestinal infections, and his stamina suffered so much that the Whalers decided to trade him.

The move, however, proved to be one of the best things to ever happen to Howe as well as the Flyers.

———

The year is 1982.

Prince William is born to Prince Charles and Princess Diana in London, EPCOT Center opens at Disney World in Orlando, Florida, and Sony launches the first compact disc player.

And it's Mark Howe's first season as a Flyer.

At the time the players had a tradition of giving each other gag gifts for Christmas in an anonymous Pollyanna gift exchange. "We all drew names out of a hat. Nobody knew who gave anybody anything, and I drew Clarkie's name [Bobby Clarke]. And I remember thinking, you know, as a new kid, this was a bad one to get," he said. "He was getting toward the end of his career. So I went to a retirement home on Route 38 and got a bunch of brochures. When he opened it up, he said: 'What's this? I don't get it. What's so funny?' He had this snarly look on his face," Howe laughs. "He wasn't too happy. I was like, 'Uh-oh,' but I wasn't saying a word. I don't think he ever knew who it came from."[56]

Philadelphia was where Howe's career really took off. His best season took place in 1986–87 when he posted some of the best numbers ever by a NHL defenseman: 82 points (24 goals—seven of which were shorthanded—and 58 assists).

During his 929 NHL games, Howe amassed 742 points (197 goals and 545 assists) and 455 penalty minutes. Howe ended his illustrious on-ice career in his beloved hometown of Detroit, where he currently serves as director of pro scouting.

He is back in the city where it all began—those many years ago on those snowy outdoor rinks.

---

56. At the time of this writing, Bobby Clarke was still in the dark as to who gave him the gift. Surprise, Dad! It was Howie.

CHAPTER 11

DAVE POULIN

Situated on the Mattagami River roughly nine hours north of Toronto, the mining city of Timmins was Canada's largest municipality in land area until 1995 and remained the largest municipality in Ontario until 2001. Being in northeastern Ontario, Dave Poulin's hometown has very cold winters, of course, but temperatures in late summer and fall tend to be among the coldest for any major city in any Canadian province.

"I can remember vividly back to grade one, grade two—when it was so cold that they would have a hard time on Monday mornings starting up the furnace at school. So you'd get the day off because it was too cold…but then you'd go skate outdoors. It was a nice irony. It was too cold to go to school but not too cold to play hockey. Maybe that goes to show the importance of hockey in Canada," he smiles.

"We always played outdoors. There was a priests' college right behind my house, and they would make up four sheets that were just absolutely perfect outdoor ice. And it was almost a graduation where there were smaller rinks where you started, and then there was the big rink where the really big, good players got to play. They had full boards around them and snowbanks literally four feet, five feet high. And there was also a lake in town called Gillies Lake, and they would set up the boards right on the lake. And there would be a number of rinks set up like that. We just loved it."

———

The year is 1967.

The major sports news revolves around Muhammad Ali, who is stripped of his World Heavyweight Champion titles and banned from boxing by the various commissions for his refusal to be inducted into the United States Army.

In basketball, UCLA wins the NCAA Championship 79–64 against Dayton, the first of an unprecedented seven consecutive titles for the Bruins. In the local basketball scene, the Philadelphia 76ers win 4–2 against the San Francisco Warriors to become NBA Champions.

And in hockey news, 1966–67 serves as the 50th season of the NHL and saw the debut of one of the greatest players in the sport's history: defenseman Bobby Orr of the Boston Bruins. The Toronto Maple Leafs win the Stanley Cup, their last Cup to date, marking the last game played in the Original Six era. And at 3601 South Broad Street, the Spectrum—home of the Flyers and Sixers until 1996—had just been built.

And Dave Poulin, age nine, moves to Toronto and begins to play organized hockey.

Although a relatively late start for most Canadian kids,

Poulin says, "I was never behind them. I learned to play on the playground—literally—because I hadn't played organized before. But I was never behind them. So any hockey experience I had was simply *playing hockey*. And when you're just playing—not being coached—you learn the game better because you have no choice.

"It's kind of funny because I think a lot of the problems with youth hockey today is that it's over-coached. Here's the expression for coaching today: it's 'graph paper coaching,' which means you have to be in an exact square of the graph paper. And that's football. That's not hockey. Think about this: every four to six seconds, they blow a whistle to stop the [football] game so they can control it and call the next play. That's not what our game is. Yes, there are set pieces. There are certainly parts of the game that need structure and fundamentals, such as the power play and special teams…but there has to be a creative side of the game versus a script. The beauty of our game is the impromptu nature of it. And that still comes from the playground.

"I think too often with the youth now, we're telling them exactly where to go in the rink, and that doesn't help our game at all. Do you think Claude Giroux only goes where someone tells him to go? No, he goes where his gut tells him to—where the open ice is, where the vulnerable spots are.…He attacks the weaknesses of the other team. So when I started playing at nine years old, I had nobody in my ear that was telling me where to go. I went where the puck was, where I thought it was supposed to go—I did what came naturally."

Because of his background in figure skating, Poulin was one of the best skaters the moment he stepped on the ice to play hockey. But because of his smaller size[57], he was often told he'd never make it to the next level.

"I would be the last player to make the team," Poulin says. "And then I would go on to lead the league in scoring, and then the next year they'd say, 'Well, you did it at *that* level, but now everyone's bigger and stronger, and you'll never be able to do it at *this* level.' The ironic thing is, I was getting cut from teams because [NHL] hockey was getting bigger, stronger, more physical. It was the Broad Street Bullies and the Big Bad Bruins. So as a 12- or 13-year-old I was getting cut because I supposedly didn't have what it took to make NHL teams that I was eventually going to be the captain of."

Poulin's hockey career started off with a bang in 1978–79 when he was playing college hockey for Notre Dame and set the record for most goals by a freshman (28) and tied the record for points by a freshman (59), records he still holds today. He stands tied for fifth on the Notre Dame career goals list (89), sixth in points (196), and seventh in assists (107). Poulin still shares the Notre Dame career records for game-winning goals (13) and hat tricks (8).

---

57. Dave Poulin is 5'11", 190 lbs.

Although his college career was remarkable, his size was still an issue for some, and he was overlooked in the NHL entry draft.

————

The year is 1983.

McDonald's first introduces the McNugget, Michael Jackson introduces the moonwalk, and the final episode of *M*A*S*H* airs, becoming the most watched episode in U.S. television history.

It's also the year the 76ers complete one of the most dominating playoff runs in league history as Dr. J, Moses Malone, Maurice Cheeks, Andrew Toney, and Bobby Jones lead the Sixers to capture their historic second NBA championship when—with 59 seconds to go—Julius Erving orchestrates a three-point play to crush the Lakers in a four-game sweep.

And, as the Phillies celebrate their centennial season, they defeat the Los Angeles Dodgers in the National League Championship Series before losing the World Series to the Baltimore Orioles. In hockey, the New York Islanders win their fourth consecutive Stanley Cup, sweeping the Edmonton Oilers.

And, following graduation from Notre Dame, Poulin finds himself playing with the Rogle hockey club in Sweden, totaling 35 goals and 27 assists and catching the eye of head coach Ted Sator, who also happened to be a scout for the Flyers.

Very impressed by Poulin, Sator set the wheels in motion, and Poulin signed as a free agent with the Flyers. In his first game, he scored goals on each of his first two shots before a hometown crowd at Toronto's Maple Leaf Gardens.

The following year Poulin joined Tim Kerr and Brian Propp to become one of the most feared offensive lines in the NHL. Right away Poulin set a franchise record for most points by a rookie (76), a distinction he still holds to this day. The following season he was named team captain, succeeding Bobby Clarke.

"What I'm most proud of is probably an intangible thing," Poulin says. "For me the thing I take the most pride in is how I would be viewed as a teammate. I played for teams that went to the final four, six times. And you look at those Flyer teams that we played on from 1982–'83 to '90…the winning percentage of those teams was unbelievable. There is now—just as of this summer—only one Hall of Famer from those teams [Mark Howe], and we were playing against Edmonton [twice in the finals] who had, what? Six or seven? It was the makeup of our teams, of being part of that group that I'm most proud of. And a lot of that came to light with [the death of] Brad McCrimmon because he was such a team guy. I think the team aspect of the sport is way better than any individual part of it. It's hard to be a successful team in Philadelphia without being passionate and matching the passion of the fans. If you think of the great teams in the various Philadelphia sports—when they were at their best—you would have to include passionate in their description."

Defying so many odds, Poulin leaves a legacy of 13 exciting years in the NHL, where he played 724 games and recorded 530 points (205 goals and 325 assists) and 482 penalty minutes, as well as a number of records and awards, and 10 years as head coach for his alma mater, where 19 of Poulin's players were selected in the NHL Draft.

So does Coach Poulin have any advice to offer?

"Don't overcoach the sport," he says. "When you're playing, there should be some freedom and creativity, and it should be left up to the kids more than it is. There should be some portion of practice that is unstructured and strictly left for the kids to play and figure things out for themselves.

"Let me give you an example: in certain areas of the country, geographically, because ice time is at such a premium, and it's so expensive, the parents feel they have to coach and structure every single minute of practice. And so the kids only do what they're told to do. So as I've presented to USA Hockey a number of times, we devised games that made the kids think. So here's an example: we would go across one end of the rink, inside the blue line, and we'd put nets on the opposite side boards. And then we'd play two-on-two across the ice, goalies in each net. But when I started doing it, I'd watch and say, 'Okay, you guys can score on either net.' Well that caused instant confusion… and you'd still have one of the blue players trying to beat two of the white team instead of simply turning and skating to the net that nobody was covering. There was no thinking of where the open ice is. What's the best option? They just thought, 'Well I'm supposed to beat the other guy,' while the best players *think* the game."

Today, Poulin is the vice president of hockey operations for the Toronto Maple Leafs, a position he's held since 2009. "In my position now the amateur scouting comes through my office," he says. "So I talk daily with the director of amateur scouting about what we're looking for. They [the prospects] can't just skate fast, or shoot hard, or be big and strong. They have to be able to think the game. Right now, for example, there's a whole wave of kids coming up who started the game by playing ball hockey, and they're just so creative in the way they play the game. And because they were handling a ball more than a puck—which is harder, of course—their stick skills are outstanding. But what's most impressive is that there's a really neat level of creativity that you just don't see anymore."

Poulin appreciates creativity off the ice as well, particularly when pranks are played.

"In Boston I played with Garry Galley[58], and he was a ring-leader. He would put shaving cream in your towel, Tabasco

---

58. Garry Galley played in the NHL from 1984 to 2001, including four seasons with the Flyers. Today he cohosts the *More On Sports* radio program on Team 1200 in Ottawa and is a color commentator on *Hockey Night in Canada*.

sauce in your red wine, baby powder in your hair dryer," he chuckles. "It was always pretty funny to see a guy flip the blow dryer on, thinking he looked pretty good after a game, and have a big waft of baby powder shoot out and cover him. Galley never, ever got caught with his fingerprints on it, though. And when questioned, his standard expression was: 'Get the *right* guy—not me.' But he was always just a little too close to the scene of the crime a little too often," he laughs.

On February 23, 2004, Poulin was inducted into the Flyers Hall of Fame.

"My route was pretty blessed," he says. "I was pretty fortunate. I had good health for the most part. Obviously I was never drafted and I was just in the right place at the right time on a lot of fronts. I wouldn't have changed a whole lot. You know what's interesting is that certainly I wish I could've had a skill set that was greater. And yet, if I had, then maybe I wouldn't have developed the work ethic that made me able to play at the highest level."

CHAPTER 12

RICK TOCCHET

The year is 1964.

It's the year when "The Hit Heard Round the World" occurs when, in a game between the Buffalo Bills and San Diego Chargers—the first of two consecutive league championships for the Bills—Buffalo linebacker Mike Stratton lays a particularly ferocious hit on Chargers wide receiver Keith Lincoln, breaking Lincoln's ribs and knocking him out of the game. It's when Philly favorite Joey Giardello wins a 15-round decision against Rubin "Hurricane" Carter to win the World Middleweight title[59].

And it is also the year another Philly athlete known for inflicting bruises, Rick Tocchet, is born.

The youngest of three boys, Rick grew up in Scarborough, Ontario, and first learned to skate at about six years old.

---

59. Though born in Brooklyn, Joey Giardello lived most of his life in the East Passyunk Crossing area of South Philadelphia where a statue stands today honoring him. Inducted into both the International Boxing Hall of Fame and the World Boxing Hall of Fame, Giardello's career record was 101 wins, 25 losses, and 7 draws. However, perhaps most impressively, he was 5–3–1 against other boxers in the Hall of Fame.

"We used to freeze the back of the schoolyard during the winter, and I remember I had an old pair of skates and I went out and learned there and loved it. It was basically just a frozen field in the back of the school. We didn't have boards. We just used snowdrifts. The only bad part was, when you lost a puck, trying to find it in the snow," he says. "My biggest memories from growing up are playing what we called road hockey with my brother Dan. I probably played more street hockey in my life in our driveway. We used to play all the time pretty much seven days a week."

Tocchet's childhood was similar to many Canadian boys. "All I ever did was play and watch hockey. *Hockey Night in Canada* was a staple in our house on Saturday nights. Eight o'clock on

---

60. Widely considered one of the most naturally gifted and popular players ever to grace the ice, Guy Lafleur's career spanned 17 NHL seasons—14 with the Canadiens alone—where he won the Cup five times. The all-time leading scorer in Canadiens' history with 1,246 points (518 goals and 728 assists), he led the NHL in points three consecutive seasons and holds the Canadiens' franchise record for most points in a season with 136. The first player in NHL history to score at least 50 goals and 100 points in six consecutive seasons, Lafleur was also the fastest player (at the time) to reach 1,000 points, doing so in only 720 games. An Officer of the Order of Canada and a Knight of the National Order of Quebec, he won three Art Ross Trophies, two Hart Memorial Trophies, three Lester B. Pearson Awards, and both the Conn Smythe and Lou Marsh Trophies. An inductee of the Hockey Hall of Fame and the Canadian Sports Hall of Fame, Lafleur is one of only three players to have returned to the NHL after being inducted into the Hall of Fame (Gordie Howe before him and Mario Lemieux after him). He still holds the record for the most career point and assist totals in Canadiens franchise history, as well as the second-highest goal total behind Maurice "Rocket" Richard. In 1998 he was ranked No. 11 on *The Hockey News*' list of the 100 Greatest Hockey Players.

Saturday night every week, we'd be watching those games. I was a Montreal Canadiens fan, and Guy Lafleur[60] was my idol. I'm pretty opposite of him," he laughs. "But he was my idol."

When Rick turned seven, his dad enrolled him in a "church league"—similar to a house league—and that's when he started playing organized hockey.

Tocchet started out playing offense, but after about the 10th game of his fledgling career, he says, "You know, I've always wanted to play goalie and was basically crying to my dad every night, 'I want to try it. I want to try it.' *Finally* they put me in. And we ended up losing the game 11–1. So that was it. It was my first and last stint as a goalie.

"I played one year [with the church league], and then there was this guy in the stands who said, 'Listen, I think you're good enough to be playing in major,' which was a better league in Toronto. So after one year in the church league, I got the chance to go and play for the Don Mills Flyers[61], which was more competitive and at a higher level."

---

61. Since its inception in 1960 when they wore white, blue, and gold and were affiliated with the Don Mills Civitan house league, the Don Mills Hockey Association has been serving the personal and hockey developmental needs of children from ages eight to 17 years of age. Then in 1968, the Rep "AAA" Clubs (as they are now known) struck an agreement with the Philadelphia Flyers, allowing the association to wear the Flyer emblem and use the orange, black, and white.

In addition to Tocchet's future Flyers teammates Scott Mellanby and Peter Zezel, the Don Mills Hockey Association also turned out NHLers Kris Draper and Anson Carter.

During his NHL career, Tocchet recorded 952 points (440 goals and 512 assists) and 2,972 penalty minutes, which also happens to be the exact number of penalty minutes he recorded during his 18 seasons in the NHL, a feat that landed him tenth on the list of the statistical leaders of the most regular season penalty minutes[62].

"I started training really seriously when I was around 13, 14, 15 years old. Then, when I got to Sault Ste. Marie [OHL], when I was 17, 18, 19," he says. "That's when I started thinking I had a shot that I might have an opportunity to get at least a crack at an NHL training camp."

But Rick's journey to the pros wasn't without difficulty. In fact, at age 17, he faced what he considers to be the biggest obstacle of his career, one that nearly ended his career before it even began.

"When I went to training camp in Sault Ste. Marie, I was at a point in my career that it could've turned out either way," Tocchet says. "Sault Ste. Marie drafted me, and I went to training camp and I got hurt the first or second day. I had a pretty serious knee injury. Back then usually you didn't have much time to prove yourself. When you'd get injured, it was usually like, 'That's too bad,' and you got sent to Tier 2, Junior B, or

---

62. The only players with more penalty minutes are Tiger Williams with 3,966, Dale Hunter with 3,565, Tie Domi with 3,515, Marty McSorley with 3,381, Bob Probert with 3,300, Rob Ray with 3,207, Craig Berube with 3,149, Tim Hunter with 3,146, and Chris Nilan with 3,043.

wherever they sent you. And I remember thinking I was going to get sent down. Because, I think I was a fifth-round pick; I wasn't any high pick. So I was very lucky that Terry Crisp and Sam McMaster kept me around. They kept me around for two weeks. And I remember that while the other guys were going through training camp and guys were getting cut, I remember sitting on the couch at the hotel with ice packs on my knee, and I said to myself, 'When I get my chance, the first time I hit the ice when I'm healthy, I've got to make that first impression because I might not get this chance again. As soon as I get out there, I have to make an impact.' And I did. I remember I went after the toughest guy on the ice, and I was going to the net hard....Whatever I had, I left it on the ice my first time back. It was to thank Terry Crisp and Sam McMaster for keeping me around, because who knows? If I go down to Junior B...who knows? I may never get a crack at it again."

But, of course, he received that chance.

———

The year is 1983.

The Washington Redskins win their first Super Bowl—their first NFL title since 1942—in a 27–17 victory against the Miami Dolphins. Miami, however, wins it all on the college stage as the Hurricanes win their first national championship over the Nebraska Cornhuskers 31–30 in the Orange Bowl.

The Baltimore Orioles—whose third baseman, Brooks Robinson[63] receives induction to Hall of Fame during the same year—win the World Series in five games against the Phillies.

And Rick Tocchet is drafted by the Flyers.

"I remember my brother called me and said, 'Let's head down to the draft.' I had heard I'd maybe go third, fourth, fifth round...I didn't even know," Tocchet says. "You just kind of hear some things, you know? And back then when I got drafted, the first day they had rounds one through six, and the second day they had six through 12. So I remember as the rounds kept going and going, my brother said in the sixth round, 'We're going to be either eating steak or hamburger, because if we don't make it the first day we have to come back the second day.' Terry Crisp was actually sitting up there in the stands, and he went down to the Flyers' table and said some good words about me and talked to Bob McCammon and Dennis Patterson and Gerry Melnyk. And he went down and came back up, and I think the Flyers had [two of the last] picks before the sixth round was over. So I got picked just before the day was over. It was quite a thrill just to get drafted, just to be able to go down to the draft table and meet everybody and go to the room after and put that jersey on, to wear the Flyers crest, knowing how prominent they were in the NHL....It was one of the greatest moments of my life to be able to say that I got drafted into the NHL by the Philadelphia Flyers."

---

63. Brooks Robinson is the 14th player elected in his first year of eligibility.

The year is 1984.

In the wake of the 1973 and '79 oil crisis and energy crises, recession continues to be a problem in the United States, and 70 U.S. banks fail in just one year. Ronald Reagan defeats Walter Mondale with 59 percent of the popular vote, the highest since Richard Nixon's 61 percent victory 12 years earlier[64].

Following the United States' boycott of the Olympic Games in Moscow four years earlier, the Soviet-bloc countries[65] boycott the Olympic Games in Los Angeles, where Mary Lou Retton becomes the first female gymnast from outside Eastern Europe to win the Olympic all-around title[66].

---

64. Ronald Reagan carried 49 states in the Electoral College; Walter Mondale won only his home state of Minnesota (by a mere 3,761 vote margin) and the District of Columbia.

65. Minus Romania.

66. After winning her second American Cup, the U.S. Nationals, and the U.S. Olympic Trials in 1984, Mary Lou Retton suffered a knee injury when she was performing a floor routine at a local gymnastics center and recovered just in time for the 1984 Summer Games. After battling neck and neck, Retton was trailing Romanian gymnast Ecaterina Szabó by .15 with two events to go. With baited breath the crowd was stunned as she scored perfect 10s on floor exercise and vault to win the all-around title by 0.05 points.

Additionally she won four additional medals: silver in the team competition and the horse vault and bronze in the floor exercise and uneven bars. For her performance that included four other medals in addition to her gold, she was named *Sports Illustrated* magazine's "Sportswoman of the Year" and appeared on a Wheaties box, the first woman ever to do so.

William Penn and his wife, Hannah Callowhill Penn, are made Honorary Citizens of the United States, while another Philadelphia legend—albeit a less historic one—Rick Tocchet, age 20, arrives in the city after being drafted 121st overall.

"I was born in Toronto, which is a big city obviously, but [being in Philly] was overwhelming. I didn't know much about Philly at all and I was very nervous. I just remember getting picked up at the airport and going over the Walt Whitman Bridge, getting dropped off at the hotel and the next day going to the hockey rink and just looking at certain players and how big they were and how they carried themselves and learning how the whole NHL thing worked....It was very overwhelming to me," he says with a smile.

The year that Rick arrived in Philly was unique. The Flyers were the youngest team in the league—with Mark Howe being the oldest player on the team at age 27—and they had a new coach, new players such as Tocchet and Peter Zezel. And they defied all odds and made it to the Stanley Cup Finals.[67]

---

67. During the 1984–85 season, the Flyers' 18th in the NHL, Mike Keenan, a relative unknown at the time, was hired as head coach and named second-year player Dave Poulin team captain. Behind the phenomenal goaltending of Pelle Lindbergh (who led the league with 40 wins and won the Vezina Trophy) combined with the prolific play of two 40-goal scorers (Tim Kerr and Brian Propp), the Flyers posted a record of 53–20–7, the best in the league that year. They went on to dominate the playoffs, first sweeping the Rangers in three games, defeating the Islanders in five, and beating the Nordiques in six, and then they found themselves in the Cup Finals up against the formidable Edmonton Oilers. Though the Flyers defeated the defending champs in Game 1 by a score of 4–1 at home, Edmonton won the next four games and ultimately the series.

So what was so special about that team?

"I played 18 years in this league. I've coached in this league," Tocchet says. "And I can honestly say that I've seen a lot of really close teams, but I don't think there's ever been a closer team chemistry-wise and we won a lot of games because of that. I don't think we won games on talent. I think we won because of the closeness of our team. Saying you love each other, a lot of people overstate that. But that's as close as you can get to when you really care for a teammate, you really care for the organization, the fans....It might sound cheesy, but I think that's why: the closeness of our team.

"You know when you have a good team, when you're on the road and you say, 'Okay guys, whoever wants to go to dinner, meet at 6:30 in the lobby.' Well I don't remember, ever, ever in those years that there were ever any fewer than 10 guys showing up. You might not have the whole team every time—sometimes guys have families and stuff—but I don't ever remember just going to dinner with one or two guys like cliques. A lot of teams have cliques. With us the least amount would be 10 guys, if not the whole team. We had a lot of team dinners. Mike Keenan and your dad [Bobby Clarke] were very big on that. Your dad and Mike Keenan would say, 'Here, take the team credit card and take the guys out to dinner.' Back then that was unheard of. And I can honestly remember 10 to 12 team dinners like that on the road, and that's unheard of. Those days are gone. And that was a big part of us winning, too. Just a simple team dinner went a long way. We'd also have a lot of fun, especially on the road. I'm a big practical joker; I love practical jokes. And on the road there'd be a lot of hijinks. We'd play all kinds of pranks. And that's what winning teams do."

Tocchet also credited the team's success in large part to the fans.

"Philly fans are very, very passionate, and I was lucky enough to get drafted to a team that wants to win at all costs," he says. "So they made sure we had the best of the best. And I was also lucky to get drafted by the Flyers because we won a lot of games, especially in those early years, and I think if you go into a losing market it might've been different. I mean, if you're in a losing environment, who knows what happens? But Philly fans in general are very passionate, and the support they give is tremendous. For me it really was quite a thrill to be able to interact with the fans. I think our building, the Spectrum, was one of the toughest places to play in sports. The way that it was constructed with the fans on top of the ice made it a very intimidating place to play. Your dad's era really made it uncomfortable for a lot of teams, and they passed the torch on to everybody else. And I think the fans have a lot to do with it. You know how they say in college football the fans are the 12th man? Well, in hockey the Philly fans are definitely the seventh man on the ice. They are *that* intimidating, and they helped us win a lot of hockey games. Like every player, I had those times when maybe you didn't feel good and you were driving to the rink and were like: 'Aw, man, I'm just not into the game' because you didn't feel well and you just try to get yourself together, to shake the cobwebs out....Well once you hit the ice at the Spectrum, the fans *made* you ready to play. So I think that was a big part of the fans that I really appreciated—that they got you ready to play no matter what."

———

Rick Tocchet met his childhood hero at an All-Star Game.

"It was Guy Lafleur's last year in the league, and he got the special invite [to the All-Star Game] by the commissioner, and the trainers there knew he was my idol and so I got to sit beside him in the dressing room. So that was pretty cool," he says, beaming.

To the disappointment of countless Flyers fans, that would be Tocchet's last full season with the team. The following year he was traded along with Kjell Samuelsson and Ken Wregget in a deal for Mark Recchi.

But Rick's career was far from over. In fact, it was about to reach new heights.

In 1992 Rick found himself in Pittsburgh, where—in 14 playoff games—he recorded 19 points (six goals and 13 assists) and helped the Penguins repeat as Stanley Cup champions.

"I've been blessed to be in a lot of great situations and see a lot of things in my lifetime," he says. "And the Cup is number one."

Over the course of the following eight NHL seasons, Tocchet would play for the Penguins, the Los Angeles Kings, the Washington Capitals, Boston Bruins, and Phoenix Coyotes, a career that would grant him the opportunity to play alongside two of the greatest players to ever play the game: Wayne Gretzky and Mario Lemieux.

"I hold it as a blessing, and I'm still friends with them today and see them quite often," Tocchet says. "Both of them really impacted my career. Before I got to play with Wayne in L.A. [1994–96] I got to room with him in '87 when we played in the Canada Cup. I remember when I went to check in for training camp and I went to get the key at the hotel front desk, and they said I was rooming with 'Wayne Douglas' because Wayne would always use different names to keep from people calling the room, etc. And when I heard I was his roommate, I was actually petrified. And I remember spending a month with him as a roommate. And just to be able to be around him and all of those older guys that won so many Cups, their presence and just being able to pick Wayne's brain on things…and his calmness after the game, it really changed my whole approach to the game, especially when it came to my mental approach. He made me a lot calmer. And then being able to play with Mario in '92 on his line and to see the talent and the numbers he put up—and obviously he was the reason I got to get a Stanley Cup ring—those experiences had huge impacts on my career, being able to play with both those guys."

In addition to winning the Cup with the Penguins, what are Tocchet's favorite career memories?

"For me the 1987 Canada Cup final game [Game 3] against the Russians at Copps Coliseum in Hamilton[68]. I've been to

---

68. The final three-game series of this tournament between Canada and the Soviet Union is widely considered the best display of hockey in history. At the time, Soviet players were prohibited from pursuing playing careers in North America, and so it was only through tournaments such as this where hockey fans could see them go head-to-head against the best of the NHL.

The tournament also was the only time the two most dominant NHL players of the last quarter century, Wayne Gretzky and Mario Lemieux, played on the same forward unit in a game of any significance, a decision made by Mike Keenan (Flyers coach at the time), and their performance will go down in sports history as probably as the best one-two punch displayed in one international tournament ever. Gretzky finished the tournament with 21 points (three goals and 18 assists) in nine games, while Lemieux had 18 (11 goals and seven assists).

In Game 2, Lemieux scored the winner at 10:07 of the second OT, and Wayne Gretzky got his fifth assist of the night, later saying that this was the best international game he ever played, estimating he played 55 minutes of the 90. And then, on September 15, 1987, with The Canada Cup in the building, the anticipation for the third and final game was almost unbearable. After two exceptional 6–5 overtime games, it just didn't seem possible the series could get any more dramatic. Well, it did. In the first period alone, the teams combined for six goals, but the Soviets headed to the dressing room with a hard-fought 4–2 lead. But the second period belonged to Canada, who scored three unanswered goals and took the lead at 5–4. Alexander Semak tied the game midway through the final period, and the game intensified as a third overtime game seemed unavoidable. Then, in a phenomenal move that dazzled the world, Gretzky moved the puck up ice after a faceoff deep in his own end. As he got to the faceoff circle in the Soviets' end he dropped the puck to Lemieux, who buried a wrister over the glove of goalie Sergei Mylnikov with just 1:26 left in regulation. Canada held on 6–5 and left the building as victors.

The exceptional skill, speed, and quality of play combined with the almost unbelievable drama and heroics led even the losing coach, Viktor Tikhonov, to call this game the most "perfect" hockey he had ever seen.

Chicago Stadium[69], but I felt Game 6 against the Edmonton Oilers in '87 and the Canada Cup game at Copps Coliseum… those two games were the loudest with the most passionate fans I've ever seen in my life. And I gotta tell you, the Winter Classic this year in Philly is definitely in my top five. I was very impressed, and it really made a great feeling for me. So I gotta put that up there. And some people say to me, 'Really? The Winter Classic?' You know, because it's not competitive like the Canada Cup or Cup Finals. But it's true. I was very honored to be invited to it, and for me it was quite a thrill; so I would say those four things. And you know, I've been to All-Star Games and stuff like that, but nothing like the alumni game [at the 2012 Winter Classic]. It was a big thing for me to see the fans— the way Philadelphia put the whole thing together was amazing. When you're skating outdoors, there's a certain feeling you get, with the wind hitting your face…when that wind hits you when

---

69. Home of the Blackhawks from 1929–1994 and the Bulls from 1967–1994, the three tiers of the famed close quarters, combined with the raucous cheers of die-hard fans and the fabled 3,663-pipe Barton organ that was played during games earned it the nickname: "The Madhouse on Madison". When the Blackhawks scored a series-clinching empty-net goal in Game 7 of the Cup Semifinals in 1971 against the New York Rangers, CBS announcer Dan Kelly marveled, "I can feel our broadcast booth shaking! That's the kind of place Chicago Stadium is right now"!

One of the last three NHL arenas (the others being Boston Garden and the Buffalo Memorial Auditorium) to have a shorter-than-regulation ice surface, as their construction predated the regulation (the distance was taken out of the neutral zone), Chicago Stadium was also the last NHL arena to retain the use of an analog dial-type, large four-sided clock for timekeeping.

you're outdoors.…I'm 47 and I remember skating out, the fans going crazy and honest to God, I thought I was seven years old again. It's hard to describe, but playing outdoors gives you the same feeling 40 years later. The sound of the puck on your stick, the ice, the acoustics of it…it's different than playing in the rinks in the NHL, and it brought me back to my childhood. As soon as I hit the ice, I felt like a kid again. But then all of a sudden, you look around, and there's 47,000 people in orange, cheering, and you're like, 'Where am I?'" he says. "When you're playing professional hockey, you're worried about winning all the time and you don't always realize the game of hockey some-times, the pureness of it."

Tocchet returned to the Flyers in 2000, contributing 11 play-off points as the Flyers reached the Eastern Conference Finals. When Rick retired after the 2001–2002 season, he joined Brendan Shanahan and Gary Roberts in becoming a part of NHL history: players collecting 400 goals and 2,000 pen-alty minutes. His regular career totals, spanning 1,144 games played, include 952 points (440 goals and 512 assists) and 2,972 penalty minutes. During 145 playoff games played, he recorded 112 points (52 goals and 60 assists) and 471 penalty minutes.

Since then Rick has been as assistant coach for the Colorado Avalanche and Phoenix Coyotes (as well as interim head coach for the Coyotes), and an associate coach for the Tampa Bay Lightning, which led to an interim head coaching position. So after 18 seasons in the league that included four NHL All-Star appearances, does this member of the legendary '87 Team Canada squad and Stanley Cup winner—and perhaps most importantly, coach, leader, and father —have any advice to offer?

"I've been in [youth sports] situations where parents are borderline ridiculous," he says. "And they're going to destroy their kids if they keep it up—not just in hockey either—even at my son's lacrosse game for instance. Just watching these parents yell and scream at the kid, or the ref, or the coach, and the intensity and the heat they're putting on the kids is going to result in your kid not liking the game. I was very lucky to have parents that loved the game. My dad and my mom…they just let me play. My dad would give me some advice every once in a while, but he wasn't on top of me, saying, 'You gotta do this, you gotta do that.' Parents need to communicate with their kids in a positive way.

"I think the No. 1 answer is to have fun, but people just throw that word out there, though, without any explanation to the kids. To me, trying *is* 'fun.' *Trying* to do something, like to be able go down the ice, go down the wing, and *try* to take the shot, or try to do a wraparound, or *try* to make two passes. To me that's fun. I think a lot of people, a lot of coaches say: 'Go have fun.' Well, what is fun? Fun to me is competition, fun is camaraderie, fun is trying your best, fun is enjoying yourself, enjoying your teammates. And I think that's lost upon so many kids who may not understand what 'fun' means in terms of hockey.

"I used to fall a lot as a young kid. When I was 11, 12, I wasn't the greatest skater, and I would fall a lot. The other kids would laugh at me, and I remember other kids, coaches, even NHL players who have said, 'If you're not falling, you're not trying.' And in hockey, you're going to fall if you're trying hard. Nobody's perfect. And kids need to know that. You fall, you get up, and you keep going. That's the way I try to live my life because you're going to fail sometimes. And I think—just like the saying goes: 'You judge a person's character *after* they fail.' How did they react? Did they get back up? Or did they just roll over and surrender? And it's the same thing in hockey."

After such a remarkable career—one that spanned nearly two decades and almost ended before it even began—what is Tocchet most proud of when he looks back?

"Wow, that's a good question," he says, taking a moment to think. "Well I guess for me personally—give or take a few other things—I think I'm most proud of the fact that I maximized the talent that was given to me. I don't think I was the most talented guy, but I think I got the most out of my talent. I really tried to give an honest effort most nights. I mean, don't get me wrong. I stunk a lot of games, too. But I was pretty conscientious of the fact that I was lucky enough to play in the NHL and with all the great players, and I loved being part of a team. So I think just in terms of myself, I'm most proud that I got the most out of my talent and had a respect for the game."

Rick's profound respect and understanding of the game is likely why he was chosen to serve alongside panelists Bill Clement, Steve Coates, Michael Barkann, and Al Morganti on the wildly popular *Flyers Postgame Live* broadcasts, a post he holds today where Philadelphia fans have embraced him since his arrival in 2010—happy to have one of their favorites back home.

CHAPTER 13

RON HEXTALL

Ron Hextall is no stranger to making history. He holds the Flyers' goaltending records for the most career games played (489), the most career wins (240), the most playoff wins (45), and the most career penalty minutes (476).

But what he is perhaps best known for is the most career points by a goaltender (28).

———

The year is 1987.

The year when Mike Schmidt of the Philadelphia Phillies hits the 500th home run of his career. It's also the year that a 24-day players' strike reduces the NFL's 16-game season to 15. The games scheduled for the third week of the season are canceled, but the games for Weeks 4–6 are played with replacement players.

And, on the night of December 8, in a game against the Boston Bruins, Ron Hextall becomes the first goalie in NHL history to shoot and score.

After a goal by Brian Propp lifts the Flyers ahead 4–2, the

desperate Bruins pull their goalie and dump the puck into the Flyers' end. Hextall plays the puck just in front of the goal line, and with a flick of his wrists he sends it soaring and slips it just inside the right post.

The Spectrum goes wild, and his teammates jump off the bench and raced to congratulate him, drawing a bench minor for too many men on the ice. It was, however, the most thrilling penalty they ever had to kill.

Amazingly, Hextall replicated the feat in the playoffs the following season.

———

The year is 1989.

It's the year Pete Rose is banned for life from baseball after an investigation concludes he gambled on baseball[70].

The Calgary Flames defeat the Montreal Canadiens in the Finals 4–2, marking the first and only time that the visiting team won the Stanley Cup at the Montreal Forum.

And on April 11 of that same year, Ron Hextall again wows

---

70. In 1991 the Baseball Hall of Fame formally voted to ban those on the "permanently ineligible" list from induction after previously excluding such players by informal agreement among voters. Then after over a decade of public denial, Pete Rose admitted in 2004 to betting on baseball, including betting on—but not against—the Reds. The issue of Rose's possible reinstatement and election to the Hall of Fame remains a controversial one in the world of sports.

the hockey world. After finishing fourth in the Patrick Division, the Flyers face the Washington Capitals in the first round of the playoffs, where the teams split the first four games. In the fifth, Scott Stevens shoots the puck into the Flyers left defensive zone, where Hexy goes around the back of the net, controlled the puck, and fires the puck into the open net, thus sealing the win—but most impressively becoming the first goalie in NHL history to score in a playoff game.

But Hexy has always been a trendsetter. In fact, it is often observed that he revolutionized goaltending with his willingness to come out of the net and play the puck, essentially playing the role as a third defenseman.[71] NHL goaltender Darren Pang described feeling as if he had "just witnessed Superman flying out of a phone booth" when he saw Hexy's puckhandling ability.

Although his coaches in juniors had warned him that if he continued to move the puck he would never reach the NHL, Hextall didn't listen and went on to establish a reputation as "the original outlet pass goalie"[72]. Martin Brodeur modeled his own

---

71. Ron Hextall's mobility was especially appreciated on the penalty kill when he provided extra passing opportunities for his teammates who, would do so to alleviate some of the pressure of the disadvantage.

72. As described by former NHL player Peter McNab (son of hockey great Max McNab) who played nearly 1,000 regular season games and went on to a career in broadcasting with SportsChannel (for the Devils) and *NHL on NBC* during the Winter Olympic games in Torino, Italy; Nagano, Japan; and Salt Lake City. In 2009 he signed a multi-year contract with Altitude Sports, where he started his 14th year as color commentator for the Avalanche.

style of play after Hextall's, saying: "I love the fact that he was playing the puck. He was one of the first goalies that came out and played the puck. He was a little rough for my liking, but it was entertaining. The playing of the puck was a big thing."

Described by the official website of the Hockey Hall of Fame as being "perhaps the game's most mobile goalie of all time," Hextall claims his adventurous approach to net minding was born early on when he played on outdoor ice rinks with a skater's stick rather than a goalie's. Although he occasionally played outdoors as a kid when it was feasible weather-wise, the bulk of Hexy's early skating experience was indoors…on the same surfaces as NHL superstars.

Arguably one of the most exciting goalies in history, Ron Hextall was born with hockey in his blood. His grandfather, Bryan, was considered one of the top wingers of the 1940s. He led the league in goals twice and in points once and scored the overtime winning goal that clinched the 1940 Stanley Cup for the Rangers. He was inducted into the Hockey Hall of Fame in 1969. Ron's dad, Bryan Jr., played in the NHL for eight seasons and was known as a fighter who could post a respectable share of goals as well. Ron's uncle, Dennis, played 681 games in the NHL during 13 seasons, totaling 503 points and 1,398 penalty minutes.

And, just as Hexy's dad first learned to skate at Madison Square Garden where Bryan Sr. was a Ranger, Ron's skating began not on a frozen Canadian pond but at the Omni Coliseum in Atlanta where his dad was a forward with the Flames.

But that's not to say he never played outdoors. "When we lived in Minneapolis[73], we had an outdoor rink right across the street from our house," Ron Hextall says. "And I was out there literally every day after school from the time I got home. Then I'd go back home for dinner, then go right back out on the ice."

Although he came from an offensively-inclined lineage—right from an early age—Ron wanted to be a goaltender.

———

The year is 1966.

John Lennon meets Yoko Ono, and The Beatles begin recording sessions for their landmark *Sgt. Pepper's Lonely Hearts Club Band* album as well as end their U.S. tour with their last-ever live performance[74], a concert at Candlestick Park in San Francisco.

The classic science fiction television series *Star Trek* debuts on televison.

The Washington Redskins defeat the New York Giants 72–41 in the highest-scoring game in NFL history, and "the Golden Bear" Jack Nicklaus becomes the first golfer to repeat as Masters champion.

---

73. Ron Hextall's dad spent his last year in the NHL between Minnesota and Detroit.

74. With the exception of a brief rooftop concert at the Apple Corps offices three years later.

And Ron Hextall, age two, is engaged in one of his favorite pastimes: throwing a rolled up pair of socks down the stairs and racing to the bottom to stop it. "Obviously there was something there at a young age that I really can't explain," Hexy said in Dick Irvin's book *In the Crease: Goaltenders Look at Life in the NHL.* "I remember going to my dad's practices, sitting behind the glass and watching the goalie the whole time. I can't explain it, can't pin-point it. It wasn't like I watched a certain guy one time and said, 'I want to be a goalie like him.' It was just there from the start."

Hexy began playing organized hockey at age eight in Pittsburgh where his father was a forward for the Penguins. "I started out as a forward, so I could learn how to skate," he says. "But then a few months into the season, our goaltender was sick. So I went in the net, and that was pretty much it."

From a very young age, Hexy knew he wanted to be a hockey player. "I was eight, nine, 10 years old, and all I wanted to do was play in the NHL," he says. "That was my focus. I can't say there was a particular moment when I said to myself, 'I have the potential to play in the NHL.' Obviously being drafted is a big moment, and you realize people are acknowledging that you at least have a chance to play in the NHL, but it was my dream all along, and I had a belief in myself.

"My dad was fairly hands-off with me. Obviously not knowing the position might have had something to do with it, but he pretty much just expected a strong work ethic and for us to enjoy what we're doing. His belief was that if you're going to do something, do it right. That's the biggest thing that was instilled in me, my brother, and my sister by both my mom and my dad: the work ethic."

But Hextall's parents never pressured him to play, just like he never pressured his own kids.

"I think a lot of hockey parents are absolutely out of their minds. I don't know how else to say it," Hextall says. "To have so much invested in your kid's sports is crazy. One in a million kids end up playing pro sports. I think for a young kid to play on a team and be a part of the team and learn the work ethic and the commitment, and everything that goes along with it is important. Playing sports and being part of a team teaches lessons that will help carry a kid through life. I think the parents that pay their kids to score a goal or go overboard in other ways…I just think the focus is a little off in what's important in life. I think to allow your child to reach his dreams is great, but to try and push a child to reach his dreams, I think people are way off. Quite frankly, I think that if a parent pushes you in hockey, and you don't become an NHL hockey player, I think the natural tendency is to feel like you failed. And I don't think that's fair to do to a kid. So I think parents should support their kids' dreams and should support whatever sports their kids choose—and certainly encourage them to play sports, but I don't believe putting pressure on your kid is productive."

And this laissez faire approach has benefitted Hextall's son, Brett, who was drafted by the Phoenix Coyotes as a sixth-round pick (159th overall) in 2008. He was signed to an entry-level contract with the team in April 2011. And if he plays in the NHL, he will become the second ever fourth-generation player in NHL history.[75] "It's his lifelong dream," Ron said. "If Brett wanted to go and be a doctor or an accountant…or go try to be the best at whatever he wanted to do, that would be fine with me as long as he's doing what he wants to do. He clearly wants to play in the NHL, though, so I'm extremely proud of what he's accomplished so far, and hopefully he can meet his goal in the end."

———

The year is 1986.

And athletes—both young and old—shine.

Mike Tyson knocks out Trevor Berbick in the second round, becoming the youngest world heavyweight-boxing champion at age 20, and Jack Nicklaus becomes the oldest Masters winner at age 46.

And after two years honing his skills in the American Hockey League (AHL) and winning the Dudley "Red" Garrett

---

75. Blake Geoffrion of the Nashville Predators was the first. His great-grandfather, Howie Morenz, was a Hall of Famer whom The Canadian Press named the best hockey player of the first half of the 20th century. His grandfather was Hall of Famer Bernie "Boom Boom" Geoffrion, who is credited with inventing the slap shot. His father, Dan, played three seasons with the Canadiens and the Jets, and his uncle by marriage, Hartland Monahan, played as well.

Memorial Award as the AHL's Outstanding Rookie of the Year, Hexy arrives in Philly and does so with a bang.

On opening night of the 1986–87 season against the Oilers, Wayne Gretzky tears off on a breakaway and comes racing toward Hexy—then just 22 years old—who drags a pad to make the save, prompting Gretzky to yell, "Who the hell are you?"

To which Hexy replied, "Who the hell are *you*?"

A memorable start to say the least. But when he looks back over his career, what is the thing Hextall is most proud of?

"When I reflect and look back, I think our team in 1987 when we went to the Finals and lost to Edmonton in Game 7 is what I'm most proud of, because we had such a great team," he says. "We weren't the most talented team, but what made our team was our heart and our desire and our willingness to sacrifice for each other."

But Hexy didn't always feel such affinity for the Flyers.

"I hated the Flyers," he says. "Bobby Clarke and company playing against my dad…I remember a brawl they had in Atlanta in the playoffs and quite honestly I remember going to a Flames game and being scared because my dad was playing against the Flyers. So I didn't like them all the way growing up…and then I get drafted by them, and all of a sudden there's this love affair. It's very ironic. But the thing is—while I didn't like the Flyers—I always respected them. I think part of the reason why people hated the Flyers or hate them today is their style of play, their passionate fans. But when you get on their side, it's what you love about the Flyers. Nothing's accepted other than winning, and the fans are passionate, and if you're not playing hard they'll certainly let you know."

Part of the 1992 trade that brought Eric Lindros to the Flyers, Hextall was traded to the Quebec Nordiques where he played one season before moving on to the New York Islanders. In 1994, he returned to the Flyers, a move that thrilled him.

"I think Philadelphia is a great sports town," Hextall says. "And I really, really enjoyed my time there, especially because of the fans."

Hextall's following seasons included recording 31 wins, achieving a goals-against average (GAA) of 2.17, which was both the best of his career as well as the best in the NHL that year. He played all 12 games of the 1995–96 playoffs, achieving a GAA of 2.13, his lowest in any postseason. Shutouts, however, were one of his greatest feats. In 1995–96 he had four, which he surpassed by nine the following season. During his first five seasons in the NHL, Hexy recorded just one shutout, but during the final six seasons of his career, he amassed 19 before retiring in 1999.

Hextall's post-playing days included stints with the Flyers as a pro scout and then as director of professional player personnel, prompting the Manitoba Sports Hall of Fame to declare him "a key factor" in the success experienced by the Flyers in the early 2000s when they won the Atlantic Division three times and reached the Eastern Conference Finals twice.

In 2006, he was named vice president and assistant general manager of the 2011–12 Stanley Cup champions, Los Angeles Kings, a position he still enjoys today, as well as serving as the general manager of the Kings' AHL affiliate, the Manchester Monarchs.

The winner of the Vezina Trophy and Conn Smythe Trophy, Hextall was the winner of the Bob Clarke Trophy three times.

In 2008, Hextall was inducted into the Flyers Hall of Fame, a place he earned by dazzling us over the course of 13 exciting NHL seasons.

Gritty, talented, and truly one of a kind, Ron Hextall left an irrefutable legacy in the world of hockey.

CHAPTER 14

CHRIS THERIEN

The year is 1975.

It's the year of the Philadelphia Oil Refinery fire as well as the year Elton John releases his hit single "Philadelphia Freedom." It's when the world is first introduced to a blue-collar, scrappy boxer from the Kensington section of Philadelphia named Rocky Balboa. And, of course, it is the year Flyers won their second Stanley Cup, beating the Buffalo Sabres four games to two.

It is also the year that Chris Therien, then a kindergartener, begins skating on the frozen ponds of his hometown of Ottawa, Canada. Little did he know then, he was embarking on a hockey career that would encompass winning a silver medal in the XVII Olympic Winter Games, 11 solid years in the NHL—10 of which included playoff appearances—as well as setting a wholly impressive franchise record: Therien holds the rank of first among Philadelphia Flyers defensemen for games played (753).

But back then, Therien just remembers feeling one thing: "I was lucky," he says. "I had three great outdoor venues where I could join pickup games and hone my skills."

———

The year is 1971.

The Phillies draft Mike Schmidt in the second round.

Football fans celebrate the Miami Dolphins victory against the Kansas City Chiefs in a divisional playoff game. This double-overtime contest is the longest game in NFL history and the Chiefs' last-ever home game at Municipal Stadium.

Football fans, however, mourn the loss of Detroit Lions wide receiver (and Philly native) Chuck Hughes[76], the only NFL player to date to die on the field during a game.

It is also the year Chris Therien was born.

As a child Therien's first choice was to play on the Rideau Canal, the largest skating rink in the world. Less than a mile from his house, he and his dad would head down after his dad got home from work. They'd play after dinner or sometimes

---

76. Born in Philadelphia, Chucks Hughes played at Texas Western College (now the University of Texas at El Paso). Still listed in the all-time football records of his alma mater; Hughes' accomplishments include:

- The most receptions in a single game (17)
- Second in all-purpose yards for a season (2,044)
- First in all-purpose yards per game for a season (204)
- Second in all-purpose yards per game for his career (132)
- Fifth in all-purpose yards all-time (3,989)
- Second in career receiving touchdowns (19) and yardage (2,882)

In 1967 Hughes was drafted back to the city of his birth in the fourth round by the Eagles and played three seasons before being traded to the Detroit Lions prior to the start of the 1970 season. Although listed as a wide receiver, he saw most action on special teams. In his five-year career he caught only 15 passes.

On October 24, 1971, in a game against the Chicago Bears at Tiger Stadium in Detroit, Hughes had run a pass route but was not part of the play;

before. "We'd both have our skates, our sticks, and our gloves," he remembers, smiling. "It was great."

Then there were the community rinks, one in each district, including his home district of Canterbury. "The City of Ottawa put boards up in each recreational park as well as a wooden hut with a space heater where we could go to get our skates on, have hot chocolate," he recalls fondly. "It was pitch black. So they would turn on lights for us. When the rink got too rough, the guy who was in charge would turn on the fire hydrant with a crank and flood the ice."

Therien's dad—an accomplished player in his own right—played juniors with Saint Mike's and could have potentially gone on to play professionally but instead opted for a scholarship to St. Lawrence University. "[He] never pressured me,"

---

an incomplete pass intended for Lions tight end Charlie Sanders. Hughes was jogging back to the huddle when he suddenly collapsed on the Bears' 15–yard line without contact. Initially some thought he was faking an injury to stop the clock, but Bears linebacker Dick Butkus frantically signaled for help on the field.

Hughes had suffered a fatal heart attack. The autopsy revealed that Hughes, unknowingly had been suffering from advanced arteriosclerosis; his coronary arteries were 75 percent blocked, and that he had been done-in by a blood clot that completely cut the circulation to his muscle. (Hughes' family had a history of heart problems.)

Hughes was buried in San Antonio, Texas, and all 40 of his Lions teammates attended his funeral, including head coach Joe Schmidt.

He was survived by his widow, Sharon Leah, and his son, who was 23 months old at the time.

The Lions retired his no. 85, in his honor, and annually make an award to the most improved player in his name. Chuck Hughes was 28 at the time of his death.

Therien says. "Of course it's every father's dream to have your son be one of the 700 players in the NHL. So everybody wants to know how I did it. Parents always ask, 'what did your parents do?' The answer is, my dad took me to the rink. He worked on things with me, but he didn't push me. He helped me."

He also built a backyard rink each year, trying to have it up in time for Christmas. "It wasn't big," Therien says. "But it was big enough for six or eight kids to play. We loved it."

In addition to the outdoor venues, Therien, at age six or seven, recalled joining his first organized hockey club called a house league. "It was freezing cold," he says. "The indoor rinks had no glass, just chicken wire."

When he returns to his hometown, he still looks for the rinks but doesn't see them as often anymore. He talks about this a bit wistfully. "Pond hockey is the foundation and essence of who we are as Canadian people," Therien says. "Everybody wanted to be Wayne Gretzky or Bobby Clarke."

What's so compelling about Therien's story, however, is that he almost did not become a hockey player at all.

———

The year is 1986.

The Space Shuttle *Challenger* disintegrates just 73 seconds after launch, killing the entire crew. The Chernobyl disaster in the Soviet Union occurs when a mishandled test at the nuclear plant kills more than 4,000 people.

Baseball has both tragic and crushing events. American League manager Dick Howser is diagnosed with brain cancer after mixing up signals during the MLB All-Star Game, and Bill Buckner[77] of the Boston Red Sox infamously lets an easy ground ball roll through his legs in Game 6 of the World Series.

Chris Therien's world is also featuring its share of disappointment. Now 15 years old, he is cut from not one—but *two* Double A teams.

"I was so discouraged," he says. "I didn't think I should've been cut."

---

77. Bill Buckner appeared in all 162 games in 1985 and batted .299 with 16 home runs and a career high 110 RBIs in the No. 2 spot in Boston's lineup.

In September 1986 Buckner hit .340 with eight home runs and 22 RBIs while missing just three games in spite of chronic ankle soreness. (Buckner became the first major league player to wear Nike high-top cleats in an effort to relieve pressure from his ankles.)

For the second consecutive season, Buckner drove in more than 100 runs for and was a key member of the team that ran away with the American League East by 5.5 games. He entered Game 5 of the 1986 American League Championship Series batting just .111 in the ALCS and was 0-for-3 in the game when he singled to start the ninth inning rally, which was capped off by Dave Henderson's famous home run. He went 3-for-6 in the final two games as the Red Sox came back from the brink of elimination to defeat the California Angels and win the American League pennant.

Despite these achievements as well as accumulating more than 2,700 hits in his 22-year career, unfortunately he is best remembered for the Game 6 fielding error, a play that has since been prominently entrenched into American sports lore.

As a result, he quit hockey for an entire year and skied instead, spending about four nights a week at the local ski club. "I wonder at times if that had an impact on me more than anything—your drive when you come back to shove it up people's rear ends or at least to prove to myself I was a decent enough player," he says.

And prove himself he did.

Just three years later, after making his comeback and spending his last two years of high school at a prep school in Lake Placid, he found himself at the NHL draft in Vancouver.

Therien says he never had any real aspirations to play in the NHL, "It was such a far reach. I never realized until I was 18 or 19, when I was in college that maybe this could actually happen. And even then, I never realized it would happen as quick as it did. And that—to me—was what was really unbelievable."

———

The year is 1990.

It is a year of upsets and surprises.

In what many consider biggest upset ever in boxing—and perhaps any sport—Buster Douglas defeats Mike Tyson by a knockout in the 10th round to win the world's unified heavyweight title[78], and the Cincinnati Reds sweep the heavily favored Oakland A's in the World Series.

In pop culture news, a McDonald's opens in Russia, in

Moscow. Pop sensation Milli Vanilli have just been outed as lip-synchers, and their Grammy award is revoked.

It's also the last time an NHL season would end in the month of May, and Chris Therien, age 18, is drafted. At the time there were only 21 teams in the NHL; today, there are 30. The Flyers had seven picks in the first three rounds. "There was speculation I could go from the late first round to not getting drafted at all that year," he says.

But he needn't have worried. They picked him 47th overall. Russ Farwell was the GM, Paul Holmgren the coach. "I was just shocked and just very, very pleased to be a Philadelphia Flyer and put that crest on, knowing the history of who that team was—already a very decorated franchise, in my eyes," Therien says. "And I was just thrilled to be drafted by them."

Getting drafted was not only thrilling but, as Therien says, "A completion of all the work I'd done and everything I'd been through, up until that point in time. It was like the ultimate reward."

---

78. On February 11, 1990, in Tokyo, Japan, Buster Douglas scored a stunning upset when he knocked out Mike Tyson—the previously undefeated champion who, at the time, was considered to be the best boxer in the world and one of the most feared heavyweight champions in history due to his utter domination of the division. The Mirage Casino in Las Vegas, the only Las Vegas casino to make odds on the fight, had Douglas as a 42-to-1 underdog for the fight.

Douglas held the title for eight months and two weeks, losing on October 25, 1990, to 28-year-old, 6'2", 208-pound Evander Holyfield, via third-round KO, in his only title defense.

An added bonus for him was that he was close enough to Ottawa so that, "If I ever made it, my parents could come down and see me," he says.

Therien started his professional career in 1994, playing for the Hershey Bears of the AHL, the Flyers affiliate, but once the NHL lockout came to an end, he joined the Flyers and played every regular season and playoff game in the abbreviated season, earning a spot on the NHL All-Rookie Team. This same year Chris was a member of the Canadian team, which won silver at the XVII Olympic Winter Games in Lillehammer, Norway.[79]

As a rookie for the Flyers, he always got to the rink an hour before anyone else and would hang around with whomever came in early. When the others arrived, they'd always find him in front of the TV, watching his favorite show, *Married...with Children*, known for its good-natured but sarcastic main character, Al Bundy. "The guys caught onto my personality pretty quickly, and they said, 'You are *just* like that guy on TV.'" And thus Therien's nickname—Bundy—was born. "The name just stuck. There were times in my career where someone would yell

---

79. In the semifinals, Canada beat Finland 5–3 while Sweden beat Russia 4–3, setting up a Canada vs. Sweden matchup for the gold. After the final period, the match was tied 2–2, resulting in a shootout. After six shots it was tied 2–2 until Sweden's Peter Forsberg beat Corey Hirsch, causing the Swedes to win after a Paul Kariya failure. This led to Tomas Jonsson, Håkan Loob, and Mats Näslund becoming the first three members of the Triple Gold Club. This is a term used to describe both hockey players and coaches who have won an Olympic Games gold medal, a World Championship gold medal, and the Stanley Cup.

'Chris' on the ice, and I wouldn't even answer. I wouldn't even know who they were talking to," Therien says.

When asked about his pregame rituals, Therien says, "Nothing really crazy, compared to what I've seen." Mainly, he'd always try to leave at the same time. "If the game started at 7:00, I'd leave the house by 3:30 in order to get to the rink by 4:00. I'd put the right pad on before the left and say a little prayer that my teammates and me would remain healthy—as healthy as we could, anyway."

While always focused and serious on the ice, off the ice was another story. "I like to think of myself as one of the kings of pranksters," he says. For example, Therien and his teammates liked to engage in what they called "shoe checking." On road trips, at the lunch meal or dinner meal, the whole team would be "in" on targeting one guy, who, unbeknownst to him, would be the designated "shoe checker."

"Someone would grab a big thing of whipped cream or chocolate sauce or ketchup and casually scoot under the table and dip it on the end of the shoe checker's shoe. Then he'd go back to his table, and everyone would start ringing silverware on their glasses. The players would look under the table, and to his amazement, the shoe checker would realize he'd been gotten and would have to raise his hand, saying, 'Yeah, you got me.'

"One day we're in Chicago. I'd been keeping my eyes on my shoes the whole lunch. I was in the clear. I go up to the dessert cart to get a little bit of ice cream, and when I get back to the table, everyone starts dinging on their glasses. I look down at my shoe, and it's got a mess of sauce and whipped cream on it. And I'm like, 'That couldn't have happened. I've been watching the whole time!'"

So Therien went back over to the dessert table and pulled back the tablecloth, and there was Andy Delmore crouched underneath, laughing.

"You're dead," Therien said as he laughed and began plotting his revenge.

They played that night against the Blackhawks, and the next day, Delmore took advantage of Michigan Avenue, the famous shopping mecca in the Windy City, and bought himself an expensive trench coat. "I think it was like $700. And he *loved* that thing," Therien says. "So to get him back, I cut the sleeves off this brand new coat he loved so much. He went to put it on, and the sleeves just came right off. We were all dying. He looked like he was wearing one of the vests from *The Matrix*. I thought he was gonna cry."

Therien, of course, denied being the culprit, and with the rest of the team laughing just as hard, Delmore probably never knew for sure who did it.

But who else could it have been but the lovable jokester, Bundy?

Therien enjoyed his best season in 1996–1997 by recording a career high in points (24) and plus/minus (+27) in 71 games while helping lead the Flyers to the Cup Finals. After playing nine and a half seasons with Philly, he was traded to the Dallas Stars on March 8, 2004, for a 2004 eighth-round draft pick and a 2005 third-round draft pick. He signed a one-year contract to return to the Flyers shortly after the 2004–2005 NHL lockout came to an end and ended up playing in 47 games before having his season cut short due to a head injury.

Known primarily for his defensive skills, Therien was usually partnered with Eric Desjardins over the years and was famous for elevating his game when matched up against star forward Jaromir Jagr.

During Therien's impressive NHL career, he accumulated 159 points (29 goals and 130 assists) and 585 penalty minutes. He is currently the Flyers color commentator and owns a company with former Flyers teammate John LeClair.

CHAPTER 15

KEITH JONES

It's no secret that Philadelphians are some of the most passionate sports fans in the world. And in December 1968, their passion got the better of them—notoriously so.

It is halftime.

After a horrible losing season, the Eagles[80] were well on their way to losing yet *again*—this time to the Vikings—and the disgruntled fans at the December game were in no mood to applaud—much less celebrate—when a crowd-plucked, make-shift Santa Claus appeared on the field to perform with the cheerleaders. This infamous event is when Eagles fans boo and jeer…and pelt poor Santa with snowballs.

It is also the year Keith Jones is born and, although he did not start off his hockey career with the Flyers, he always enjoyed playing in Philly mainly because of those fans.

---

80. Their 36th season in the league, the Eagles failed to improve on their previous output of 6–7–1, winning only two games, and well on their way to having an anti-perfect season at 0–11, until they finally won their 12th game. They were the only team in the NFL to lose 11 consecutive games in one season since the 1936 Eagles, though in the AFL the 1962 Oakland Raiders lost their first 13 games.

"I always liked coming into this city, because when I came as a visiting player, it was always at the Spectrum," he says. "And it was always so incredibly *intense* that it *literally* forced you to play harder than you may have ever felt like before you stepped on the ice. I found it to be really great motivation then—as 'the enemy'—and then even better motivation as a Flyer. I came to Philadelphia with great anticipation, and I was not disappointed in the least when I arrived. Philly is a place like no other."

But let's go back to when it all began.

"My early memories of playing were all outdoors," Jones recalls. "And I just remember having a blast doing it."

———

The year is 1972.

The American classic *The Godfather* is released in cinemas, and the first ever *New Year's Rockin' Eve* airs on ABC with host Dick Clark.

On the sports front, the 1972 Summer Olympics serves as a watershed event. While records were broken, tragedy also ensued. Israeli athletes and coaches were taken hostage by Palestinian terrorists, and 11 Olympic team members were eventually killed.

Swimmer Mark Spitz of the United States has a spectacular run in 1972, winning seven Olympic titles and setting seven world records.[81] However, being Jewish, Spitz is forced to leave

Munich before the closing ceremonies for his own protection after fears arise that he may be an additional target of those responsible for the Munich massacre.

In the final of the men's basketball, the United States loses to the USSR, in what USA Basketball calls "the most controversial game in international basketball history"[82], ultimately resulting in the U.S. team refusing to accept their silver medal, which remains held in a vault in Lausanne, Switzerland.

And Jonesy, then a four-year-old, is beginning to play in his first league called the Park League at a rink right outside the school he attended from kindergarten through eighth grade—where all the parks would play against each other.

"All the schools had a park that had monkey bars and a playground in one area, as well as a tennis court and such in the other. In the winter the parents would get together and flood the tennis courts. They would put wooden boards up around the fence, and they'd put nets out that had no mesh on them. They would just hang up blankets over top of the goal posts and the crossbar, and that would serve as your netting in case any little guys wanted to try and cheat and shoot it through the back," he says with a smile.

---

81. The seven world records in a single Olympic meet were tied by Michael Phelps in 2008.

82. In a close-fought match the U.S. team initially believed it had won with a score of 50–49, but confusion over a late timeout gave the Soviet team a few seconds to score two more points and claim victory.

"We wore tuques [ski hats]—no helmets—and would skate all day [typically 10 or 12 hours]. The beautiful part of it was as soon as your game ended—as long as there wasn't one after—you could skate all that you wanted, and there was always a pickup game. The winters seemed a lot harsher then, at least as far as the amount of snowfall, at least where I grew up [about an hour west of Toronto]. I have great memories of being so cold getting there, but as soon as you'd hit the ice, you'd warm up right away.

"And when you weren't playing, you were sitting in built-up snow banks on either side of the ice. Those were our benches, and I'd stay until they shut the lights off. Then I would skate two blocks home on the frozen roads."

As he grew up, he began to play indoors. "You always hear parents telling their kids, 'When I was your age I used to walk 30 miles in the snow, uphill…both ways,'" he says. "But for me it was actually true. I used to walk to the arena—which was then called North Park but is now the Wayne Gretzky Sports Center—with my equipment bag over my shoulder and head up there for the 5:00 AM practice, and I remember thinking I was never going to make it, even though it was only a handful of blocks."

Although he did walk frequently, it wasn't as common as his dad waking him up and taking him there. "The early mornings were the biggest obstacle, because your hands would be so cold and hurt so bad that the parents ended up tying our skates," Jones says. "And as a father now, I can't imagine it being a whole lot of fun, getting up at four in the morning and taking some grumpy kid to the rink. But all the grumpiness went away as soon as we hopped on the ice. And our parents stood there—and I'm sure froze—as they watched us. It was a great commitment by all the parents who had a kid involved in hockey."

Brantford, Ontario, sometimes known as "The Telephone City[83]," is the birthplace of Wayne Gretzky, *Saturday Night Live* comedian Phil Hartman, and former Flyers right winger Jonesy.

When asked what it was like to grow up in the shadow of "the Great One," Jones, almost eight years younger than Gretzky, says: "Gretzky then was royalty in the hockey world, just as he is today. So for a player like I was, it was never a realistic thought that you'd ever be Wayne Gretzky. But he just made the game so magical to watch that I think—without question—there was an influence in attracting young players, including myself to want to play in the National Hockey League.

"I think that he somehow allowed you to keep your own aspirations realistic because he was *so* great that you looked around and saw some of the players that played with Wayne—oftentimes considered obscure players in some people's minds…until they played with Wayne. Then all of a sudden they were put on the map. And I think more than anything I thought, 'Boy, I'd like to be one of those guys who played with someone like Gretzky and could be a complement to a player who's that great.'

---

83. Alexander Graham Bell, a former resident, conducted the first long distance telephone call from the town to Paris, Ontario, in 1876.

"So from that standpoint, he definitely had an influence—a rather direct influence. Of course I probably followed his career closer than anyone else's growing up," he says. "No. 1, because he was the best; and No. 2, because he was from my hometown."

When asked at what point it occurred to Jonesy that he might have a real chance of playing in the NHL, he laughs *hard* and says, "To be honest with you, it was the day I met with the scout from the Washington Capitals, a guy named Jack Button. That was the first time."

———

The year is 1987.

Canada introduces a one-dollar coin, nicknamed the "Loonie." President Ronald Reagan challenges Soviet Premier Mikhail Gorbachev to tear down the Berlin Wall.

And Keith Jones, age 19, is playing Junior B hockey in Niagara Falls, watching the NHL as a fan, believing any shot to play pro has disappeared, since he already had one year of draft eligibility go by. "I was just a fan of the game, going to Maple Leaf Gardens and never once thinking I would be on that ice someday," he says. "I figured that time had already gone by. I was almost in shock when he [Jack Button] told me he was with the Washington Capitals and potentially they may want to draft me in the upcoming draft. And so that's when I started to think,

'Well, hey, maybe there *is* something here,' and then everything seemed to fall into place from there."

In 1988, Jones was drafted in the seventh round, 141ˢᵗ overall and began his NHL career playing with the Capitals, where one of his most humorous locker room memories took place.

"Dale Hunter and Calle Johansson were the two biggest pranksters on the team. And Calle had this Swedish fish—it's considered some kind of delicacy in Sweden," he says. "I'm not sure, because after my inaugural experience with it, I never looked much into it. And so anyways, this fish—this putrid fish—it came in a jar, and when he took the lid off, it had the most horrific smell you could ever imagine. But I had never been introduced to it before this day.

"So one day I came out of practice and I was kind of curious as to why Dale and Calle were still hanging around…and as I walked out [of the rink] to my car, they had these looks on their faces like something was up. And as I got to my car, I smell this *smell*…but to be honest, it wasn't even in the category of smells; it was a million times worse. And I remember thinking, 'Why is there a garbage disposal around my car?' It was just terrible. So I was in a hurry to get away from it—whatever 'it' was that was surrounding my car. So I jump in and as I backed out of my parking spot, I saw them both poke their heads out of the door of the rink, and at that same moment, I got a whiff of this thing that was beyond a stink. Oh my God, I can't even describe just how bad it was. Nobody should ever have to experience that smell, and because they were both poking their heads out of the door, I knew something was up and threw my car in park and jumped out. And as they laughed, I investigated until finally underneath my driver's seat, I found this little garbage bag that had been folded over a bunch of times with this supposed Swedish delicacy in it—this horrible, horrible fish. I grabbed it and threw it out of the car as fast and as far as I could…but trust me when I tell you it took me at least 10 days to get the smell out. And not just 10 days of airing it out naturally like with the windows down and stuff. *No*. It was 10 consecutive days at the car detailer, paying to get that stink out. I had to drive with my head out of the window it was so bad. Because they hadn't just laid a dead fish in a trash bag. No, that wasn't enough—they'd rubbed it all over the handles of the car, the steering wheel, the mirrors, the rugs—on every part you could imagine. It was brutal," he laughs.

"They did it to a bunch of other guys, too; the prank was so good. But one of the guys was real anal about how clean his car had to be all the time, and after it had been done to him he went into this…*rage*…and basically threatened to kill everybody unless someone confessed," he chuckles. "It was a very interesting couple of days in that locker room."

————

After 491 NHL games, accruing 258 points (117 goals and 141 assists) and 765 penalty minutes, Jonesy then transitioned into a very successful second career as a sportscaster. He currently works as an in-studio TV analyst for *NHL Live* on the NBC Sports Network, as a color commentator and analyst for Comcast Sportsnet and The Comcast Network, as well as a cohost with Al Morganti, Angelo Cataldi, and Rhea Hughes weekday mornings on the radio at 610 WIP in Philadelphia. He's also the coauthor of his autobiography, *Jonesy: Put Your Head Down and Skate*.[84]

The best advice he received from a coach came when he was playing Junior B in Niagara Falls. "There was an associate coach that used to come in sometimes and help us out," Jones says. "And his name was Mark Botell, who, ironically enough, actually played in a handful of games with the Flyers.

"He was a big, tough defenseman that also played Junior A hockey in my hometown of Brantford. I didn't know him then, but he came back and volunteered to help with the [Junior B] team in Niagara Falls because he lived there and he would come out and work us extremely hard in practice. And it really was one of the first times I'd had in junior hockey that were concentrated on conditioning, and believe me, I wanted to quit halfway through most practices, but he kept pushing.

"Anyway, one day he just kind of took me aside, and I remember he had me over for dinner with his wife and his family. And he had a puck on a plaque on his wall with the Flyers

---

84. Cowritten with EPSN SportsCenter anchorman John Buccigross.

emblem on it, and it was his first goal in the National Hockey League. I don't think he had many more after that, and if I'm not mistaken, your dad [Bobby Clarke] had an assist on it. And it was on his wall, and I just remember looking at it and then him looking at me and saying: 'It's not unrealistic that if you put the work in, that you could get the opportunity to one day play—or one day score—in the NHL.' And that stuck with me. I used to call him when I was in college—he was like a mentor—and whatever minor problem I had at the time that I thought was major, he would keep me focused on what the ultimate goal was."

Looking back, Jonesy's perspective is very straightforward, "The best advice is given a lot," he says. "But it's not followed a whole lot. It's not about making it to the NHL as much as it is about having fun and enjoying every level that you play at.

"You can enjoy things in life in a lot of different ways; one way is being successful at something. The other is not necessarily being the best player but being a player that can make *other* players around them better. Better players become great when they have guys around them that can contribute to their success.

"It's not always about being the best player on the team; it's about being the best player *you* can be. Oftentimes parents become frustrated that their son or daughter is not 'the best' on their team—whatever the sport. And that doesn't mean, for example, that your son is never going to play in the NHL. That's just not true. Look at me.

"If I look back on my childhood and my hockey memories, if I'm being realistic about placing myself in the picture of most teams I played on, I was always in the middle of the pack. And in that role, I was allowed to just be *a* player. I didn't have to be '*the* player.' And I think that served me well as I weaved my way through my minor hockey career and then my professional career.

"So I think that letting your kid develop athletically at his or her own pace is really important, and the less the amount of pressure you're putting on him or her, the better."

CHAPTER 16

KEITH PRIMEAU

The year is 1976.

And Keith Primeau is five years old, just beginning to play organized hockey outdoors.

In present day, Markham, Ontario, lays claim to being "Canada's Hi-Tech Capital," a hospitable northern host to a number of international corporations such as Apple, Honeywell, IBM, Lucent, Motorola, and Toshiba.

But 35 years ago, it was simply a place where young Keith Primeau honed his skills. "I lived in Markham till I was 10. And the elementary school I went to when I was six, seven, eight, nine years old used to freeze the schoolyard into a little rink, and I would be there by myself, playing until it got dark," he recalls. "And I knew when it got dark, I had to be home. So I would take my skates off and walk through the park and the forest to get home all by myself, and I think about it now. And I'm like, 'I'd never let my kids do that,' but that's what we did."

Growing up, Primeau's dad was his biggest influence. "Not only because he was my father, but also because he coached me all the way through every year except for one when he went to

195

coach my younger brother Wayne[85]," he says. "He had the biggest impact on me as a player and as a person."

His dad's best advice?

"As a player the strongest message he sent all had to do with consistency and determination," Primeau says. "As a person it was all about integrity. It's the most important thing regarding who you are as a person. That's what people will remember you by, and that's more important than any game or any sport."

———

The year is 1985.

Wearing Cinderella's slipper, Philadelphia-based Villanova defeats favored Georgetown 66–64 to win the first 64-team NCAA Tournament.

Locally, Philadelphia Mayor Wilson Goode orders city police to drop an explosive into the radical group MOVE's headquarters, killing 11 MOVE members and destroying 61 surrounding homes. On a more positive note, the hugely popular *Live Aid* pop concerts in London and Philadelphia raise over £50 million for famine relief in Ethiopia.

And Keith Primeau is 14 years old and playing hockey in

---

85. Also an NHL player, Wayne Primeau was drafted in 1994 by the Buffalo Sabres and scored his first NHL goal in his first NHL career game against Martin Brodeur of the New Jersey Devils.

Communist Russia, where Mikhail Gorbachev was just named general secretary of the Soviet Communist Party and de facto leader of the Soviet Union.

"It was a pretty neat experience," Primeau says, remembering fondly. "Adam Foote[86] played on that team as well."

Primeau's team was on a 20-day hockey trip that also included playing in Finland and Sweden, but the most memorable game took place in St. Petersburg, Russia. "We got dressed at the hotel and were bused to the game," he says. "It was nighttime, and it was five-people-deep around the outside [of the rink]. So it was pretty exciting initially. We started off with a big lead in the first period.

"The benches were dark, but we could see a lot of commotion going on over on their bench. And as the game wore on, the Russian players started getting bigger, and stronger, and faster…until eventually they took over. And by the third period, they were all different. They must've gone through 60 kids, trying to win no matter what, filtering in as many kids into the game as they could, ending with the best players."

The start of Primeau's professional career might be best summed up in an old cliché: he was in the right place at the right time.

---

86. Two-time Stanley Cup winner (with the Colorado Avalanche); three-time captain with the Columbus Blue Jackets; gold medal-winner in the 2002 Winter Olympics, and World Cup Champion with Team Canada in 2004.

"I was playing major bantam AA hockey when I was drafted into the Ontario Hockey League at 15 years old," he says. "I had the opportunity to play in a tournament in British Columbia where there were several scouts, and after they saw me, they started calling back East, asking who this Primeau kid was, and I had the opportunity to go to the under-17 tryouts. There was still another week of that, and a bunch of the teams showed up to see me skate. And from there I was drafted by Bill LaForge to the Hamilton Steelhawks.

"My first year of junior, I played both Junior A and Junior B, and my second and third year I started to put up numbers."[87]

But was becoming an NHL player anything he considered a possibility?

"We all aspired to play in the National Hockey League," Primeau says. "But I don't know if any of us really understood whether or not it was realistic. My dad's goal was for me was that if I could get a college scholarship out of it, then it [hockey] was a bonus.

"But once I was drafted to play juniors, I knew that that was what I wanted to do. And that became my main priority and my focus. And I had three years before my draft year, and that benefitted me. Going into my third year, my draft year, I was

---

87. In 160 games, Keith Primeau had 194 points (83 goals and 111 assists) and 222 penalty minutes. He was named Second All-Star Team OHL and won the Eddie Powers Memorial Trophy for Leading Scorer OHL.

mentioned in that class [1990]—with Mike Ricci and Owen Nolan and Petr Nedved—but I was kind of on the outside. I wasn't there yet.

"But I was determined I was going to be mentioned in the same sentence as those players. And that's what drove me all year."

———

The year is 1999.

Football fans celebrate the Denver Broncos winning their second consecutive Super Bowl, defeating the Atlanta Falcons 34–19, and they also mourn the death of the legendary Walter Payton.

It's the year Lance Armstrong wins his first Tour de France, as well as *The Fight of the Millennium*, when Felix Trinidad defeats Oscar de la Hoya to unify the IBF and WBC's world Welterweight championships.

And golf fans are wowed by the British Open, as they witness the epic collapse of French golfer Jean van de Velde as he throws away a three-shot lead on the final hole, finding himself in a playoff, which Paul Lawrie won, and they mourn the untimely of Payne Stewart in an air accident.

And in hockey news, the last game played at the historic Maple Leaf Gardens is marked with a Blackhawks win, while the Dallas Stars defeat the Buffalo Sabres to become the first team from the southern United States to win the Cup.

And, after nine years in the NHL playing for the Detroit Red Wings, Hartford Whalers, and Carolina Hurricanes, Keith Primeau becomes a Flyer.

"We [NHL players] all knew the reputation of the Philadelphia sports fan, the Philadelphia hockey fan," Primeau recalls. "It was like a circus; there were always stories coming out of Philly. It was one of those teams—whether it was the aura, or the history, or the tradition, I don't know, but Philly was always media fodder. So when I found out I had the opportunity to come play [here], I looked forward to the challenge. And once I arrived, I knew right away it was where I was meant to be."

His only regrets?

He recollects them a bit pensively, "I just wish I could have arrived sooner and I wish I could have stayed longer. Because it was the one place on my tour that I really felt as though the people understood me and who I was as a player."

After all, Primeau's most memorable experiences in the NHL happened during his time as a Flyer. The first one dates back to the year 2000, the year in which Wayne Gretzky's No. 99 jersey was retired league-wide, and it's the inaugural year of the Atlanta Thrashers.

And at the 92:01 mark of overtime, Keith Primeau takes the 130th shot of the game to score the Flyers' game-winning goal in the fifth overtime against the Pittsburgh Penguins in the unforgettable Game 4 of the Eastern Conference Semifinals.[88]

Just four years later, the Flyers are within one game of the

Stanley Cup Finals, and Keith Primeau is leading the charge with 16 playoff points (nine goals and seven assists). "This was probably the most enjoyable game of my entire career," he said. "It was when everything came together for me at a pinnacle [Game 6 against Tampa Bay]. Offensively, I was everywhere. It was at home in front of the home crowd, and it's a game I'll always remember forever."

You probably remember it, too.

With just 1:49 left in regulation, Primeau scored the game-tying goal, saving the Flyers who then went on to win in overtime, and sending the series back to Tampa Bay for Game 7.

Hockey icon Phil Esposito would later tell Keith, "During the '04 playoffs when you and the Flyers took the Lightning to seven games, you were the most dominating player I ever saw— more than [Bobby] Orr, [Gordie] Howe, Gretzky, or anyone."

"It was a great run, and I really thought we were destined to win," Primeau recalls. "It's funny because in both years we lost in the conference finals—the year we lost to [New] Jersey after being up 3–1 in 2000, and going into Tampa Bay against the Lightning in Game 7—throughout each of those series, I remember talking with a few of the guys as we watched the Western Conference. And we all agreed the winner of the East was going to be the Stanley Cup winner. All we had to do was

---

88. The game ran 152 minutes and one second, the longest game in modern NHL playoff history. It started at 7:38 PM and ended at 2:35 AM EST.

get out of the East and we'd have a real opportunity to win the Stanley Cup. And of course, eventually, both teams that we lost to went on to win the Cup.

"There's no guarantee that we would have won, but I felt strongly that the best team was in the East, and so those were definitely devastating losses."

But even with those disappointments, Primeau has nothing but genuinely good memories when it comes to his time in the Orange and Black.

In fact, he says, he was never a much of a prankster…but when he came to Philly: "My whole mood, demeanor, and personality changed considerably when I got here because of the cast of characters I played with," he chuckles. "When I first got here, the locker room had Ulf Samuelsson, Keith Jones, Chris Therien, Rick Tocchet, and Craig Berube…and that group of guys was pretty lighthearted and really knew how to enjoy the locker room. It was different than what I'd seen up until that time. It was all in good fun, of course, but it was a real eye-opener for me.

"One guy who seemed to take a lot of the brunt of the abuse—especially from Chris Therien—was Daymond Langkow. And I remember the time we were in Buffalo, and they Super Glued Daymond's shoes to the ceiling of the locker room. Everybody thought it was hilarious, of course…except for obviously Daymond."

And how did he get them down?

"Well, he eventually whacked them down with a stick," Primeau said. "But that was part of the joke. He wasn't tall enough to get them down."

Often very dedicated athletes go to great extremes either to get equipment or to get to a game, and Keith Primeau is no exception. "I was always serious, and I was always early. Guys would just be going down for their pregame nap, and I was already headed to the rink. I was out the door by three o'clock—just as my kids were getting home from school—for a 7 or 7:30 [PM] game. Either way, it didn't matter. I just did so much preparation," he says. "So one time we're in Florida, and a good friend of mine wanted to give me a ride to the rink. Instead of me taking a cab, he was going to pick me up. And this particular day, Todd Fedoruk was up [awake] as well, and he decided to catch a ride with us instead of going with another group of guys who planned to take a cab about an hour later.

"So we're driving to the rink, ready to play against the [Florida] Panthers, and 10 minutes into the ride, my friend turns to me and said: 'This car's been pretty good. I haven't had any problems with it.'

"And I just looked over at him and said, 'You did *not* just say that.'

"And he's like, 'What? What?'

"But I didn't say anything more. And wouldn't you know it? Within about five minutes, we're stopped at a red light. And it turns green, and we're about to go and his car sputters to a stop.

So now Todd and I have to get out—in our suits—and push the car through the intersection. We had to push it to get it started again. So we got it started and we thought everything was good. We're all like, 'Whew, that was a close one,' and then…a couple of minutes later, it sputters to a stop *again*. So here Todd and I are, in South Florida, pushing this car in our suits, and it was late in the year—literally game 81 or 82—in 80-degree heat, pushing this car to get to the game.

"So by the time all is said and done, we arrived at the rink at 5:30 (PM] for a 7:00 game. We arrived *after* the guys who were leaving at 4:00 in a cab, *after* the team bus…and I wasn't happy. It messed up my routine.

"But, the best part of the story is that it was the first time Fedoruk ever had three points in a night.[89] He had a *career* night. So the joke was always that we had to have a car stall out in order for him to have such a good game."

During Primeau's 15 seasons in the NHL (909 games) where he accumulated an impressive 619 points (266 goals and 353 assists) and a whopping 1,541 penalty minutes—not to mention his playoff appearances (128 games played, 57 points,

---

89. A notorious enforcer, Todd Fedoruk played his first seven professional seasons with the Flyers organization, making his NHL debut during the 2000–01 season. In 220 games over four seasons, he recorded at least 100 penalty minutes in each season. Perhaps most notably he had titanium plates permanently embedded into his face to repair injuries caused to him during a fight with Minnesota Wild enforcer Derek Boogaard during the 2006–07 NHL season shortly before he joined the Flyers.

and 213 penalty minutes)—he's learned a thing or two. And his advice to aspiring hockey players is simple: "Enjoy the game because, soon enough, the game becomes serious…and so does life," he says. "So enjoy it while you can. It doesn't last like that forever. You're only young once. And the pressure parents put on their kids to perform and excel…well, I suppose they do it for different reasons…but it's most important that your kids enjoy competition whatever sport they decide to play."

CHAPTER 17

DANNY BRIERE

Coeur...
Heart.
Déterminé...
Determined.
Fidèle...
Loyal.
Intrépide...
Fearless.

No matter what language you use, Danny Briere encompasses all of these virtues and so many more.

The year is 1980 when another fearless and determined Canadian athlete makes history. Terry Fox, age 21, begins running his famous Marathon of Hope, a cross-country run to raise money for cancer research three years after his right leg was amputated due to the very same disease that had invaded his bones. Using an artificial leg, he runs every day for 143 days, amassing 3,339 miles[90] before being forced to quit when the

---

90. Basically the equivalent of running a marathon every single day; mileage-wise, it is roughly the distance from Miami to Seattle.

cancer spreads to his lungs. Fox's efforts lead to raising $23 million as well as being given the Lou Marsh Award as Canada's top athlete. Named Canada's greatest hero by a national survey, there have been countless entities named in his honor, including streets, highways, schools, athletic centers, fitness trails, a Coast Guard icebreaker, and a mountain.

And Danny Briere, then just three years old, is first learning to skate.

"I started skating outside on our above-ground pool when it would freeze in the wintertime. But as I got older, in the years after, my parents would build a rink for me in the backyard. People don't realize what a commitment that can be. My parents shoveled it off every time it snowed. And they'd hose it off at night before they went to bed, so there was another layer of ice, and they'd have to get up in the morning before going to work to hose it down again, so the ice would be nice for when I came back from school. I think my mom—when I was at school—she would also hose it down, and then we'd play after school and all day on the weekends. Kids from the neighborhood would come over, and we'd either skate or play with our boots…I spent *a lot* of time there in my parents' backyard," he recalls fondly.

"My parents never pressured me to play. They put so much work into that backyard rink, and all the time, the amount of travel, all the money that they put toward my hockey…following and helping out…But it wasn't for any other reason than my love of the game and their love of their son. My dad was always a huge hockey fan. So it was fun for him…but I don't think early on my mom was a hockey fan to start with. She just wanted to support me.

"Parents have to realize that it's okay to give your kids the tools to succeed, but they have to chill out at the games. They should be enjoying that time because it goes by so fast. Parents should be enjoying watching instead of screaming and yelling. There's a coach that's there for that. The worst thing you can do is overcoach. If you give advice on top of what the coach is saying, you're giving two different directives to your child, and that screws up things in his head, because the coach is saying one thing and you're saying something else. So you're already a distraction to your son when you're telling him what to do, and sometimes people don't realize that.

"For me the most telling thing is that when I look back at all the kids I played hockey with—growing up and in minor hockey—when I look back, most, if not all, of the kids that were yelled at from the other side of the ice, today they're not involved in hockey at all. They're not coaching, their kids are not playing, and they don't play themselves. The kids that were there having fun and playing for the love of the game—and their parents were just there chilling basically—today they're still involved in hockey. They're playing in a men's league, they're coaching their kids, some of them are referees…somehow they're still involved. Because it was fun, and that's what it should be."

Briere was four or five when he began playing organized hockey. "It [playing professional hockey] was always my dream from as early as I can remember," he says. "That's always what I wanted to do, and I always said, 'That's what I will do.'"

But it wasn't until 10 years later, that it actually occurred to him that he might actually be able to play professionally.

"At 14 I started thinking that it was getting closer," Briere says. "But I was still so much smaller than everyone else, and everyone kept telling me that I'd never be able to play at the next level, whatever it was. So when I was peewee, they said, I'd never be able to play bantam.When I was bantam, they said, I'd never be able to play midget and so forth. So it was almost on a year-to-year basis for me."

————

The year is 1994.

It's the 75th anniversary of the NFL but both the NHL and MLB are experiencing labor setbacks. The NHL regular season is shortened due a 103-day lockout, and the World Series is canceled due to an ongoing strike by the Major League Baseball Players Association, marking the second time in history that the Fall Classic was not played. The Montreal Expos and the New York Yankees hold the best records in their leagues at the time, and the Expos are on track to win the third consecutive World Series for a Canadian team.[91] Some have blamed the strike for the ultimate demise and relocation of the Expos,[92] as they were forced to trade numerous players to deal with the loss of revenue following the strike, and the franchise was never able to reach the same level of success it had in 1994.

And Danny Briere is 17, playing his first year of junior hockey.

"It was then when I realized that maybe I had a chance [to play in the NHL]," he says.

During his rookie season in Drummondville, Quebec, Briere recorded 123 points (third overall) and was awarded the Michel Bergeron Trophy as Rookie of the Year as well as the Marcel Robert Trophy as Scholastic Player of the Year. "The year before I was debating between college hockey and junior hockey. I was always a decent student," Briere says. "School was always very important to me. It was always a priority. Hockey was my love, but school was my priority."

The following season he recorded an additional 163 points, earning the title of league's leading scorer and the coveted Jean Beliveau Trophy that came along with it, as well as the Ford Cup for Offensive Player of the Year. Briere also was named the QMJHL Humanitarian of the Year. Always humble, Briere says, "That award was for helping out with a few things in the community. I was lucky."

---

91. Following the Toronto Blue Jays' back-to-back wins in 1992 and 1993.

92. After the 2004 season, MLB moved the Expos to Washington, D.C. and renamed them the Nationals.

And his desire to make a positive difference in the world around him continues today, as Briere's philanthropy includes founding two admirable North American charities.

"In Canada I have the Daniel Briere Foundation, and the mission for that is to give back to kids in need in whatever area that they need," he says. "We have a golf tournament every year, a poker tournament, a dinner show...and that's mostly run by my parents and my friends back home. In the past nine years, we've raised over $600,000.

"In the States I have The Briere Bunch, which I started when I was in Buffalo. And the funds that we raise from that go to Camp Good Days[93]."

In 1996 the Phoenix Coyotes drafted Briere in the first round (24th overall), making him the first player taken by the Coyotes since moving from Winnipeg. Briere, however, returned to Drummondville for one final season where—for the third consecutive year—he finished in the top three in league scoring (130 points) and was awarded the Frank J. Selke Memorial Trophy as the Most Sportsmanlike Player.

Also during this season, Briere found himself in Switzerland at the World Junior Championships, an experience that he says is one of his favorite hockey memories. "I grew up watching it

---

93. Camp Good Days provides camping opportunities, retreats, activities, and services for children, adults, and families who have been affected by cancer and other life-threatening illnesses; all services are free of charge.

on TV on Christmas in Canada," he says. "That's what everybody watches. So I was always hoping that one day I'd have the chance to represent my country. Beating the Russians in the semifinals and the Americans in the final…we couldn't have asked for a better setup. We weren't the most talented Canadian team that's ever played the world juniors, but it was just the way we formed a team.…That's when I started realizing how you don't really necessarily need to have the best players; you need to have the best *team*." Briere scored six points in seven games, helping Team Canada to win the gold medal (his second).

The additional gold medals he won in 2003 and 2004 at the World Championships are great memories, too. "It's always an honor to represent your country. So they're special, too," Briere says. "But the world junior is probably the most special of them all."

Briere split his first four seasons in the NHL between the Coyotes and their AHL affiliate, the Springfield Falcons.

In 1998, his first professional season, he was awarded the Dudley "Red" Garrett Memorial Award as top rookie with 92 points in just 68 games and was named the AHL's First Team All-Star center. To this day Briere still holds the title of third-leading scorer in Falcons franchise history.

That year also marks one of the more humorous stories of his career. "There's a lot of funny ones, but the one that sticks out was when me and my roommate, Trevor Letowski—we were both rookies—we were on the road, and we went to dinner. And while we were gone, the guys stole our key, went into our room, stole all our luggage, took out all the light bulbs in the room, put the mattresses, the dressers, the TV—everything—all against the walls, all in one corner…But the worst part—the part that is a little less PG—was in the bathroom," he chuckles. "In the toilet bowl, they emptied a roll of toilet paper…and then someone left a 'package' right on top of it, above the water. So…hours later when we walked in, there's no lights anywhere so we couldn't see anything. Everything was dark…and worst of all it stank. It was horrible. That was a good one."

After earning a consistent NHL spot on the roster in the second half of the 2000–01 season, Briere made headlines when he began a rather unconventional off-season strength training regimen with World's Strongest Man competitor Hugo Girard, who is also from Danny's hometown of Gatineau.

"You know what was cool about that was that it was so different," Briere says. "My whole life since I started training—and most of the players to this day—for the most part, you train in the gym. And you do whatever everyone else is doing, and you try to adapt it a little bit more to hockey… where this was where I was basically training the same way those strong men do in the competitions that we see on TV, where they pick up the big, huge rocks; the cars; pull the airplanes; the sleighs. We had a huge warehouse, and it was very,

very old school, but it was cool. Everything you did was for time or distance. So you always had a goal and something to beat instead of just doing reps with a certain weight. So it was really cool."

At the 2002–03 trade deadline, the Coyotes traded Briere to the Buffalo Sabres, where he would eventually become captain, and where he emerged as an NHL force to be reckoned with in his second full season with the team, recording 58 points in just 48 games in 2005–06. And despite missing 32 games with an abdominal injury that required surgery, he came back to help lead the Sabres to their first postseason berth in four years.

This is also where he found himself receiving two nicknames.

The first, "Cookie Monster," was given by longtime Sabres announcer Rick Jeanneret. "When you'd score a goal top-shelf, he'd always say, 'That's where Mama hides the cookies.'" Briere says. "And there was a game, where I think I scored two or three goals in the same area, and he called me 'the Cookie Monster,' and the fans kind of jumped on it. But I can't really say that my teammates ever really called me that."

The second, "Sneaky B," was given to him by teammate Chris Drury. "He gave it me because of the way I play, always kind of hiding behind the defensemen or on the side of the net," Briere says. "And I guess being smaller than everyone else, you're lighter and you can kind of hide a little bit more."

Speaking of size…since he was a kid, much has been made

over Briere's[94], but for all the talk, he has an interesting per-spective. "I'm not so sure that if I had been 6'1" or 6'2" and over 200 pounds like most players are," he says. "I'm not sure I would have succeeded in attaining my dream, because being smaller and being told all the time that I wouldn't be able to make it has been my motivating factor. And I still use it today. I still—every time I go on the ice—I try to prove people wrong. So if I didn't have that [adversity to overcome], I don't know how it would've turned out. I'm convinced it made me better."

Briere became an unrestricted free agent in 2007 and signed with the Flyers, who at the time had just finished the previous season as the worst team in the NHL.

"Coming to Philly [as an opponent] was always one of the toughest places to play. I grew up cheering for Montreal, and I remember [Ron] Hextall going after [Chris] Chelios in the playoffs, and that's the kind of image that's always stayed with me: the bruiser image, the Broad Street image that most people have still today. This was always one of the toughest places to play. In Philly you feel like you're enclosed, like everyone's on top of you, and they seem like very angry fans," he says. "One of the pictures that always stayed with me is Tie Domi in the penalty box when a fan falls in, and they start fighting...so that was kind of the image I had of Philly coming in.

---

94. At 5'10" and 180 pounds, Danny Briere is relatively small by NHL standards.

"Now that I'm on the inside, I *like* the reputation of the Broad Street Bullies....I *like* the fact that a lot of players still have that image when they come and play here; I think that's a little bit of an advantage [for the Flyers]. The Philly fans are very comparable to Canadian fans; how they support the team, and how important the Flyers are to this city, to the people here. And that makes it special—a lot more special than playing in a city where they don't care much about the team."

During his first year with the Flyers, Briere finished second in team scoring (72 points in 79 games), recorded his third career hat trick, and along with fellow new acquisitions Scott Hartnell and Kimmo Timonen, helped the Flyers rise from the basement of the league to an appearance in the conference finals against the Penguins. Briere had nine goals and seven assists in 17 postseason games.

The following season, however, Briere was plagued by injuries. "When you're hurt, the frustrating part is that you feel helpless," Briere says. "You're watching your teammates and you can't do anything to help—that's the part that stinks the most. You're going to the gym every day and trying to rehab, trying to get ready to come back, and you have good days and bad days. And when you have a bad day, it's very depressing. You go home and you feel like you're letting everybody down. And there's a lot of those days, especially early in an injury."

And although Danny was able to come back from injury

after injury—often in record time—that is not what he is most proud of in his career thus far.

What is it, then, that's he most proud of?

"Being able to make a difference still," Briere says. "We always hear: it's one thing to get to the NHL, but it's another thing to stick there for a long time. That's probably what I'm most proud of—that and the fact that a lot of people had doubts about me, and I was able to prove them wrong. It's not like it happened overnight for me. It wasn't an easy road to get here. I always had to fight for everything."

For proof of this, no one need look further than Briere's sensational 2010 postseason when he played his heart out and led the entire Stanley Cup playoffs in scoring (30 points, 12 goals, and 18 assists), setting a new Flyers franchise record.

Perhaps most impressively, however, he came within just one point of Gretzky's record of highest output in the Finals[95], recording the greatest Finals output since Mario Lemieux in 1992.

But, of course, the Flyers came up short and had to endure watching the Chicago Blackhawks skate around the Wells Fargo Center ice with the coveted Cup high in the air.

"Losing was tough to accept—very tough," he says. "But at the same time, it [the series] was something to be proud of. There were a lot of good things. It was an amazing series, and

---

95. Briere finished with 12 points (three goals and nine assists) vs. Wayne Gretzky's 13 points.

I think the hockey was really good. But when it [losing] happened, it was really tough. You wake up, and from one day to the next…it's all over. There's no going to the rink anymore. There's no practice to go to.…It makes for a long summer. There's a lot of wondering, you know, what went wrong, getting so close, and why it didn't work."

To this day the sting of losing has not left Briere. In fact, he still hasn't seen the overtime goal in Game 6.

"At some point I'm sure it's going to happen that I'm going to be watching a clip, and it's going to be there," he says. "But so far every time it comes up, I turn my head. I still haven't seen it, and I really don't want to see it."

Briere's performance, though, was something to watch during the 2012 playoffs. He had a pair of two-goal games in the first round, as the Flyers defeated the Penguins in six games. He became the first player in Flyers history to record three multiple-goal performances in the team's first seven games of a playoff year.

But following that long summer after the 2010 Stanley Cup, he says, "I couldn't wait to get back on the ice and get the next chapter going. My goal and the only thing I'm still looking for is the Stanley Cup. The personal records and the awards are nice, and they're something, I think, when I'm all done playing hockey that I'll probably look back on, but for right now the only goal is the Stanley Cup. I want to be able to share that with my teammates, with this organization, and with the fans."

And speaking of Philadelphia sports fans, Briere jumps to their defense when they're criticized. "They're just passionate, passionate about their teams," he says. "And to me there's nothing wrong with that. Yes, maybe sometimes they cross the line a little bit, but it's just like us playing with emotion. We cross the line sometimes, too. I've crossed the line and been suspended for it. But at least I can look back and say I played with passion. And that's what our fans have. And if you ask most players in any sport, they'll probably tell you they'd rather play in front of passionate fans than passive fans.

"Philly is amazing. Everywhere we go, people talk to me about the Stanley Cup. And it's 35 years later, and people still remember all the players and their numbers, where they were at the time—how they skipped school to go to the parade—and it's amazing. And they just can't wait for that next parade, for that next Stanley Cup to come back here."

He then smilled, a bit coyly, a bit hopefully…and a bit mischievously, too.

"And either can I," he says.

CHAPTER 18

CLAUDE GIROUX

The year is 1988.

It is the year of the first night game at Chicago's Wrigley Field, as well as when Mike Tyson knocks out Michael Spinks in Atlantic City and defends his undisputed heavyweight championship.

It is also the year that fellow standout athlete Claude Giroux is born.

Giroux grew up in the town of Hearst, a small Canadian community whose primary industry is forestry. With mills and tree-planting organizations, it was named to honor William Howard Hearst, then the Ontario Minister of Forests and Mines and later Premier of Ontario. An anomaly in Ontario—a province that is overwhelmingly English speaking—85 percent of Hearst's population claims French as its primary language.

And it's also where young Claude first began to skate.

"I used to go to public skating with my dad when I was maybe two or three years old. It wasn't an outdoor rink, but I loved just cruising around. One of my best friends had an outdoor rink that his dad would set up. It was just a small town that I was from. Hearst only has about 6,000 people, so my buddy had the only outdoor rink in the town. So we just played there from when I was maybe seven years old till I was about 13, and those lake games were always the most fun. There was no limit on how long you could stay on the ice. So we could be out there the whole day. All the older kids from the neighborhood would come over to play on weekends, and the games would get tight, and it'd get a little chippy....There'd be some fights, of course, 'cause it's hockey, but no big fights—just some slashing and some scrapping. There were no rules, and it got rough out there, because we were kids and we hated to lose. But more than anything, we just had a lot of fun," he says.

"I moved to Ottawa when I was 14 where there's outdoor rinks...pretty much everywhere."

Claude experienced a bit of nostalgia for those days gone by when he played in 2010's Winter Classic against the Bruins.

"I had the chance to play in Boston, and you're on the ice and you don't really hear the crowd because they're so far away," he says. "So you're just kind of playing the game as if no one's watching. And it's not distracting at all. It's perfect. It's just like you're in a bubble and just playing against a team that you don't like, and nobody's watching. That's kinda the feeling that you get, and it's like when you were a kid."

Growing up, Claude's idols were Doug Gilmour and Steve Yzerman. "Those two were my two favorites. I always liked Canadian teams. I was a big Montreal fan. I also liked Toronto and Vancouver. The Canadian teams would play the Flyers a lot in the playoffs, and sometimes the Flyers would kick my team out of the playoffs. So I hated the Flyers, pretty much," he says.

In 2003–2004 Claude played minor midget AA for the Cumberland Barons where, in 39 games played, he amassed 59 points (31 goals and 28 assists) as well as 28 penalty minutes. Following this success he made the jump to Junior A, and during this first junior year he was slowed down by mononucleosis. Despite the illness, he was still able to tally 40 points in 48 games[96] as well as claim Rookie of the Year honors in the Central Junior A Hockey League.

———

The year is 2005.

During Super Bowl XXXIX, the Patriots defeat the Eagles 24–21 in Jacksonville, Florida, becoming the first team since the 1997–98 Denver Broncos to win consecutive Super Bowls.

The Chicago White Sox sweep the Houston Astros to win the World Series for the first time since 1917.

It's also when Tiger Woods defeats fellow American Chris DiMarco at the first playoff hole to claim his fourth Masters title and his ninth major, while Lance Armstrong sets a world record by winning the Tour de France for the seventh consecutive year.

Although a bout of mononucleosis didn't stop Claude from

---

96. 13 goals and 27 assists.

scoring, he was forced to miss several games, causing him to be snubbed by every single team at the Ontario Hockey League's annual draft.

His luck would soon turn, however, when the Gatineau Olympiques invited him to their training camp.

Not surprisingly, Giroux made a splash from day one. During the 69 games of his rookie year, Claude recorded 103 points—including 39 goals. Over the course of the next three dazzling years, he garnered three sensational 100-plus points seasons (103 in 2005–2006, 112 in 2006–2007 and 106 in 2007–2008) and led his team to the league's championship in the playoffs, helping the Olympiques clinch a coveted spot in the revered Memorial Cup tournament.

"My coach in juniors, Ben Groulx, really helped me," Giroux says. "He's the one who pushed me to work harder on and off the ice. I was always the laziest guy...and while I had skills, I didn't have the work ethic to go with it. And I remember this one time he told me: 'If you work hard, your skill is just going to catch up to it. If you go in the corner and work the hardest, your skill is going help you win the battle.' So that always stuck with me. I had skills but wouldn't work hard...I was pretty much undisciplined. But I loved the game. I'd do anything to play. And it's not that I didn't want to work hard—not at all—I just didn't know how. And he taught me how to do that. [Fellow teammate at the time] Max Talbot would probably tell you the same thing: Coach Groulx would find a way to push you."

CLAUDE GIROUX

The year is 2006.

Barry Bonds hits his 715th career home run, passing Babe Ruth for second place on the career list and setting a new record for left-handed hitters, while Los Angeles Lakers star and Philly native Kobe Bryant, age 27, scores 81 points in a win over the Toronto Raptors, becoming only the second player in league history to score at least 80 points in one game.

And Claude Giroux, age 18, is drafted by the Flyers in the first round, 22nd overall.

Giroux made his NHL debut on February 19, 2008 in a game against Ottawa, when he was called up for two games to help the Flyers, who were plagued by injuries.

Between 2006 and 2008, Giroux bounced between the Olympiques, the Phantoms, and the Flyers, before landing himself a permanent gig in the NHL during the 2008–09 season, where he recorded 27 points in 42 games played with the Flyers.

"I've never really worked hard, never really worked out. I always ate bad. But when I went to juniors…that's when I realized I had a chance and so I started working out hard." But Claude admitted he still didn't shake his poor eating habits. "It didn't really matter to me what I ate. You know, when you're 20 years old, you don't really care. But since two years ago, with my trainer, I've been working out pretty hard and I think when you eat well you just feel better, you get more energy. And I can

227

really see the difference out there [on the ice]."

And because of this change of lifestyle, it is likely no coincidence that Giroux really came into his own during the following season. Perhaps what was most memorable was his playoff performance, beginning with his five-hole, game-winning goal on Henrik Lundqvist in the shootout against the New York Rangers that propelled the Flyers into the 2009–10 playoffs, and continuing into the first round, where Claude was a key point producer and helped dismantle the No. 2 seed Devils.

The next series the Flyers made a historic comeback. Being down 3–0 against the formidable Boston Bruins, the Flyers' hope for a run for the Cup seemed all but dashed. But with Claude's contributions, they were able to astonish the sports world and win the next four straight games to topple the Bruins before then going on to dominate the Montreal Canadiens in the following round.

The Flyers were now in the Finals, but despite Giroux's efforts and exemplary play—including the game-winning goal in overtime of Game 3 against the Blackhawks—the Flyers eventually lost in Game 6. In spite of the loss, Giroux ended up with 21 playoff points, securing his standing in the NHL as a force to be reckoned with.

Although it's undeniable Giroux's playoff exploits helped the team earn the Prince of Wales Trophy,[97] it is 2010–11 that is widely considered his breakout season, where during 82 games, he recorded 76 points (25 goals and 51 assists) and 47 penalty minutes. His 2011–12 season was even better. Giroux finished third in the league with 93 points (28 goals and 65 assists). That assist mark ranked as the second best in the NHL.

And now that he's a Flyer—a team-favorite even—how has this formerly devoted fan of Canadian hockey changed his perspective?

"Anytime you see fans that are dedicated to their team, that want their team to be successful," he says. "It is just a bigger motivation to want to play better and work harder to be successful. And I like that about Philly."

But hard work isn't the only thing on Giroux's agenda. In fact, when it comes to locker room pranks, Claude admits, "I'm usually more of an instigator. There's so many, but just a basic one is you cut your buddy's laces so when he's in a hurry to go on the ice and then pop! He's gotta get a new lace, and he's late for practice, and Coach kinda gets mad at him."

When Claude looks back over how his career has taken shape, he emits just one thing: gratitude.

---

97. Also known as the Wales Trophy, the Prince of Wales Trophy is an award presented by the NHL to the Eastern Conference playoff champions, prior to the final series of games for the Stanley Cup. Named for Prince Edward, Prince of Wales, the trophy was first presented in the 1925–26 season to the champion of the first game in Madison Square Garden and then subsequently presented to the champion of the NHL playoffs. However, throughout its history, the trophy has been awarded for eight different accomplishments, including the NHL regular season champions, the American Division regular season champions, the East Division season champions, the Wales Conference regular season champions, the Wales Conference playoff champions, and the Eastern Conference playoff champions.

"I was pretty lucky to have my parents," he says. "They both played broomball in their twenties, and they never forced me to play hockey. They never gave me [a hard time] if I played a bad game….They just kind of went with it, and anytime they could give me advice they would, but they would always let me do my thing, and I was pretty lucky for that."

And we Philly fans feel lucky as well to have Claude working as hard as he does night after night, continuing to show new and ever-more creative moves, superior plays, and, as some observers have called it, his "press box eyes"—named because he seems to see the whole ice in ways other players don't.

It's been nothing less than a privilege to witness how he's taken the hockey world by storm, doing "his thing," as he so humbly calls it…so it's probably not a stretch to say that Philly fans only really have one thing to say right now about No. 28:

Dear Claude,

It's sure going to be fun watching you succeed.

Sincerely,

Philadelphia

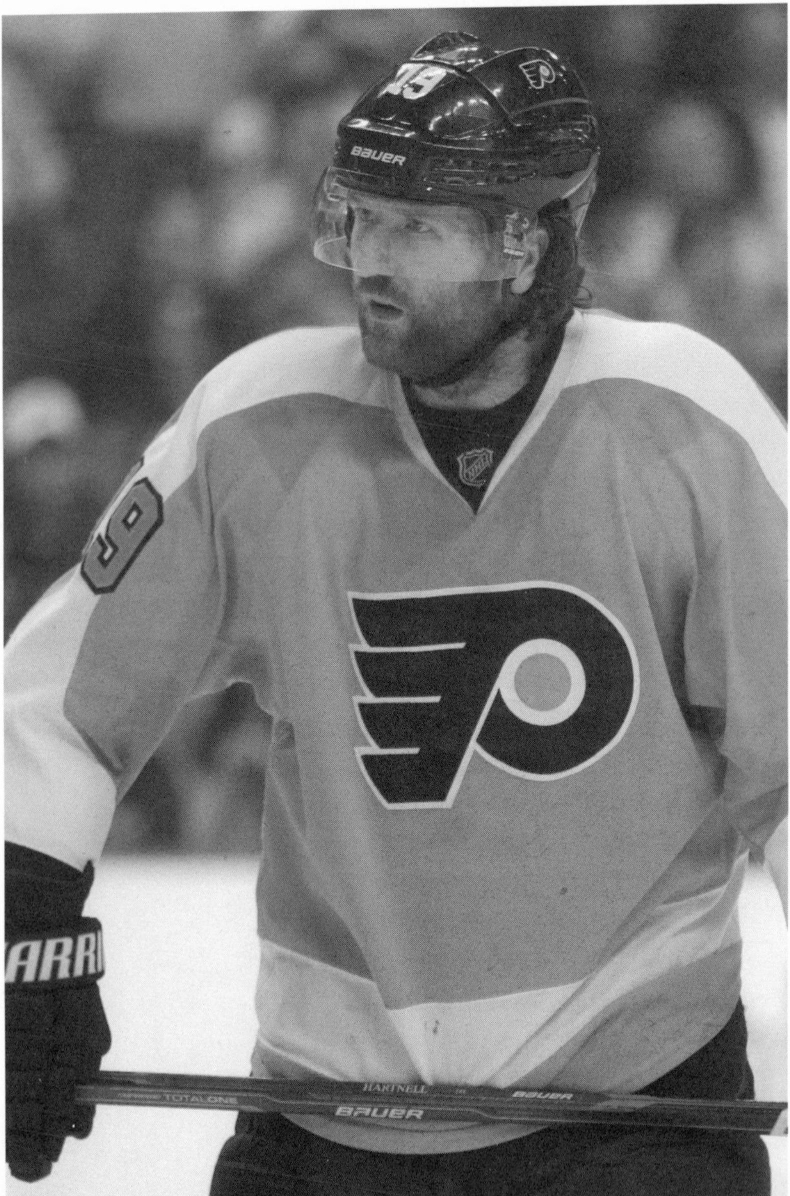
BAUER
HARTNELL
TOTALONE
BAUER
BAUER

CHAPTER 19

SCOTT HARTNELL

"I grew up idolizing my brothers and idolizing the top players in the NHL," Hartnell says. "And I always said to my dad and my family that I wanted to play with the best in the world. It was a passion inside of me. I love coming to the rink, lacing up my skates every day, and you know, you gotta sometimes pinch yourselves, because we have one of the best jobs in the world— to go out and entertain, knowing you have a whole city behind you, such a passionate city. You gotta do what you love and love what you do. And since my older brothers were my idols, I wanted to do whatever they did."

What they did was play hockey...and so young Scott Hartnell did, too.

————

The year is 1985, and it features records broken and interesting debuts.

Former Phillie and Cincinnati Reds player/manager Pete Rose breaks Ty Cobb's all-time Hit Record of 4,191 hits[98] with a single off of San Diego Padres pitcher Eric Show[99] (the winningest pitcher in Padres history). WrestleMania[100] debuts at Madison Square Garden.

Rollie Fingers breaks Sparky Lyle's American League record of 232 saves; and the Kansas City Royals defeat the St. Louis Cardinals in seven games, becoming the first team to win the World Series after losing the first two games at home.

Canadian paraplegic athlete and activist Rick Hansen sets out on his 40,000 km, 26-month-long "Man in Motion Tour" to raise money for spinal cord research and other worthy quality of life initiatives.

And Scotty Hartnell is just three years old and heading out to a rural frozen Saskatchewan pond to learn how to skate.

---

98. Ty Cobb was later found to have a career record of 4,189 hits.

99. On July 7, 1987, Eric Show hit the year's eventual MVP, Andre Dawson, in the left cheekbone with a fastball during a game. Dawson had homered in three of his last five plate appearances at that point, and the Cubs reacted with a bench-clear. Show and his manager, former Phillie Larry Bowa, later denied that the pitch was deliberate, though Bowa acknowledged it was understandable that the Cubs would think it was.

100. The first annual professional wrestling event produced by the World Wrestling Federation was viewed by over one million fans through closed-circuit television, making it the largest showing of an event on closed-circuit television in the United States at the time.

101. Scott's brothers, Chad and Devon, both earned scholarships and played Division-I college hockey, and Hartnell says: "They're probably my biggest supporters. We have a real close family, and whenever I go through tough times, or kinda get in a slump, on or off the ice, they're always there for me. And when I get too big of a head sometimes, they're not afraid to bring me back to planet earth, either."

"We lived in a town of about 800 people [Eston], where probably almost every family had keys to the rink," he says. "My brothers were probably six and eight[101] and I was maybe three years old, with the double blades strapped on, and that's when I learned to skate. It was natural ice, and we'd go out there and wheel around, and not that I was the fastest or anything, but I think it helped getting on the ice that early."

Two years later, at age five, Hartnell began playing organized hockey. "I remember my first organized game: we were five and six years old playing seven- and eight-year-olds in a little town called Dinsmore [in Saskatchewan], and we lost 45 to nothing," he says. "And I remember, we were so happy because I skated the puck over their blue line one time. And I got back to the bench, and my mom was coaching at the time, and I remember being all excited saying, 'Mom, did you see that? I made it across the blue line!' I should've called it a career then," he laughs.

Along with another lady, Hartnell's mom coached Scott's team the first few years he played. "When my parents get together with all their friends from that era," he says, "they always laugh, remembering how when teams would come to play us, they always loved coming over to shake hands with our coaches because they were the best smelling coaches in the league.

"I'd watch my older brothers play, and when I was eight, we moved to Lloydminster where there was a big junior team. And I was one of those kids—you know, when the players are coming out of the tunnel—I was one of those kids high-fiving them and asking, 'can I have your stick? Can I have your stick?' I idolized them," he smiles, remembering.

"I got Rock 'Em Sock 'Em videos with Don Cherry as a Christmas gift, and they were the best things ever. I'd watch them two or three times a week with my family or my buddies."

Roughly 150 miles from Edmonton and 2,300 miles from Philadelphia, Lloydminster has the unusual geographic distinction of straddling the provincial border between Alberta and Saskatchewan, but unlike similar cases, Lloydminster is not a pair of twin cities on opposite sides of a border. It is actually an incorporated single city. Hartnell remembers growing up like many Canadian kids with Wayne Gretzky as an icon. "Living so close to Edmonton when the Oilers were in their heyday, we'd get out on the pond, and there was always a little scrap as to who got to be Wayne Gretzky. 'I'm Wayne Gretzky.'

"No *I'm* Wayne Gretzky,'" he laughs.

The most important thing about playing pond hockey versus organized? "The amount of time on the ice was the biggest thing.

"You'd go there [the pond] right after school till dinnertime. And right after dinner was done and the dishes were put away, it was right back to the pond, and we [about eight or 10 guys] would try to get a few hours in before total darkness. Everyone would take turns playing goalie, because that was the fun position to play when you were a little kid. You got to make the big saves. I remember when I was about eight or nine during an organized game when the goalie got sick after the first period. So the coach came and asked who wanted to play net. Mine was the first hand up. So I strapped on his pads and everything. But after I let in a few five-holers, I said, 'That's the last time I want to be goalie.' I was a lot better forward than I was a goalie. It was my first time and last time."

In addition to playing on the ponds, Scotty and his friends played a lot of street hockey as well. "On our street we had probably 10 or 12 kids around my age, and when we didn't get to the pond, we'd be playing street hockey till dark. Then everyone would throw their outside lights on and light up the driveways, so we could keep going, trying to squeeze another half hour out of it. Everyone would be in snow pants and toques and mitts, and the balls would get pretty hard after a few hours out there. So nobody wanted to play goalie too much then without pads."

———

The year is 1993.

Randy Myers saves 53 games for the Chicago Cubs, breaking Dave Righetti's record for southpaws, while Lee Smith breaks the all-time save mark by recording his 358th save in a 9–7 win against the Los Angeles Dodgers.

National League teams, the Colorado Rockies and Florida Marlins play their inaugural seasons as Major League Baseball expands for the first time in 16 seasons, and Joe Carter[102] hits the second ever walk-off home run to win the 1993 World Series—the first by an American League player—lifting the Blue Jays to defeat the Phillies in six games.

And Scott Hartnell is 11 years old.

"[It was around this time when] I was able to get moved up to peewee," he says. "Obviously I was a little bit bigger—taller, more physical—than other kids in my grade, a little bit better skater, things like that. So I was moved up and played Single A hockey and learned how to body-check a year before other kids

---

102. Hailing from Oklahoma City, Joe Carter played 16 MLB seasons but is most famous for hitting a walk-off home run to win the 1993 World Series for the Toronto Blue Jays.

While attending Wichita State University, Carter was named *The Sporting News* magazine's College Player of the Year in 1981 but left that same year, and the Cubs drafted him with the second pick of the first round.

Carter first reached the majors two years later with the Cubs only to be traded to Cleveland, a move that proved to be a blessing as Carter blossomed into a star, emerging as a prolific power hitter, hitting as many as 35 home runs in a season and regularly driving in 100 or more runs. He usually hit nearly as many doubles as he did homers and would get respectable numbers of triples in many years, too. He was also a skilled base runner, stealing 20–30 bases a year with a high rate of success. In 1987, Carter became a rare member of the single-season 30/30 club for home runs/stolen bases.

However, he was considered a below-average defensive outfielder, and despite having a strong 1989 season, Carter was traded to the San Diego Padres. Although he continued to drive in runs, he also continued to have defensive problems, and the Padres subsequently dealt him to the Toronto Blue Jays along with Roberto Alomar in exchange for star players Fred McGriff and Tony Fernandez.

Emerging as a team leader, Carter's overall game improved dramatically in 1991, as he helped the Toronto Blue Jays win the division title and hit

my age did and played Double A the following year and did really well."

It was about this time when Hartnell's time spent playing pond hockey came to an end. "School was always a priority in our family, and between that and practicing a lot more [in organized hockey], there wasn't much time left to play around," he says. "Then you hear about the Bantam Draft, which happens when you're 15 years old when the Western Hockey League drafts you. It's not as big as the NHL draft obviously, but I heard I was going to go as a high pick. I think

---

the game-winning single that clinched the AL East Championship.

The following year he helped the Jays win the World Series with two home runs—their first championship as well the first ever won by a Canadian-based team and recorded the final out of the Series, taking a throw to first base from reliever Mike Timlin to nab Otis Nixon of the Atlanta Braves.

The next year the Blue Jays reached the World Series once again ready to take on the Phillies. In Game 6 with the Blue Jays leading three games to two, Carter came to bat with one out in the bottom of the ninth, the Blue Jays trailing 6–5 and two men base. On a 2–2 count, Carter hit a three-run walk-off home run off Phillies pitcher Mitch Williams (against whom he was 0–4 in his career) to win the World Series, only the second time a World Series has ended with a home run (the other being in 1960, when Bill Mazeroski did it for the Pittsburgh Pirates against the New York Yankees). It was the only time the home run has been hit by a player whose team was trailing in the bottom of the ninth in a potential championship clinching game.

Carter has the unique honor of being the first person to score a run in a World Series outside of the United States (Game 3, 1992 World Series) and the last person to do so (Game 6, 1993 World Series), a distinction that will remain in place until Toronto wins the American League pennant again. He is also the only player ever to both record the final out in one World Series, and secure a series-clinching walk-off hit in another.

I ended up going seventh to the Prince Albert Raiders, so that was a pretty neat thrill."

In addition to being captain of the Raiders—during three seasons (128 games)—Hartnell tallied 127 points (37 goals and 89 assists) and was named team MVP. He was also chosen to play for Bobby Orr in the CHL Top Prospects Game.

"Going to my first camp at 16 and moving away from home, meeting a new family for billets—you're pretty young and you don't really know what's going on," he says. "So that was a pretty eye-opening experience."

———

The year is 2000.

America Online announces an agreement to purchase Time Warner for $162 billion (the largest-ever corporate merger), the Dow Jones closes at 11,722.98, and the NASDAQ Composite Index reaches an all-time high of 5,048, evidence that the dot-com bubble has reached its peak.

In the hockey bubble, two expansion teams—the Minnesota Wild and the Columbus Blue Jackets—join the NHL, while Jaromir Jagr (of the Pittsburgh Penguins) wins the Art Ross Memorial Trophy as the NHL's leading scorer during the regular season, and Chris Pronger (of the St. Louis Blues) wins the Hart Memorial Trophy for the NHL's Most Valuable Player.

And Scott Hartnell, recently drafted by the Nashville

Predators sixth overall, is the youngest player in franchise history as well as the youngest player in the NHL. He's also about to play his first professional game—in Tokyo, Japan.

"Not many people can say that they played their first NHL game outside of North America—let alone Japan," Hartnell smiles. "So that was pretty cool. I think I might have played maybe six or seven shifts that whole game, but it was just really cool. Jaromir Jagr was there. Mario Lemieux was there. It was a huge arena, and I just remember looking around thinking, 'Wow. This is pretty exciting.'

"I only played probably two games in Philly [coming in as opposition with Nashville], and I remember one of those was a fathers trip. Our fathers came with us, and while we were getting ready for the game, our dads took a little tour of the city to the art museum, the Rocky statue, the Liberty Bell, and all the stadiums…I think Philly is the only big city in America to have all four stadiums for major sports in one area of the city, which is really neat. I heard a lot about it afterward from my dad. I asked him how it was, and he said, 'What a neat city with the history and everything—just a super cool city.'"

In his first three seasons in the NHL, he played 232 games and recorded 91 points (28 goals and 63 assists) as well as 260 penalty minutes.

During the 2003–2004 season, he recorded three game-winning goals, two of which occurred in overtime, as well as tying the team record of playoff points (three) in his first career playoff series.

Then during the 2004–05 NHL lockout, Hartnell played in Europe, helping Valerenga win the Norwegian Championship with 12 goals in 11 playoff games, earning the award for playoff MVP.

When the NHL got back into the swing of things for the 2005–06 season, so did Scott Hartnell, recording a career high of 48 points (25 goals and 23 assists), which included his first career hat trick.

During six seasons with the Nashville Predators totaling 436 games, Hartnell had 211 points (93 goals and 118 assists) and 544 penalty minutes[103].

In 2007, along with Kimmo Timonen, Hartnell was traded to the Flyers, where he immediately signed a six-year contract. That same year he scored his 100th career goal and just two days later recorded his first career natural hat trick, scoring three goals in a row. Nine days after that, he scored another hat trick, including the game-winning goal.

The following season Hartnell scored two more hat tricks within nine days of each other and posted career highs in all offensive categories with 60 points (30 goals and 30 assists) during 82 games. He also led the league in minor penalties (54).

The season after, Hartnell's playoff performance alongside Danny Briere and Ville Leino helped lead the Flyers to their

---

103. A Predators franchise record. Scott Hartnell holds another Predators franchise record for fastest two goals scored by an individual (23 seconds).

first Stanley Cup Final since 1997. During 23 games Hartnell recorded 17 points (eight goals[104] and nine assists).

Hartnell had another strong 2011–12 campaign, recording 67 points (37 goals and 30 assists). His 37 goals ranked eighth in the NHL.

Known as a gritty power forward who rarely backs away from a fight, Hartnell also skates so hard to the net that he sometimes crashes into the goalie, often drawing a two-minute penalty for goalie interference.

"A funny story that happened to me had to do with my style of play….You might call it reckless at times," he chuckles. "I'm not sure when I'm going to be falling down on the ice, sticks flying everywhere, things like that…so in Nashville they taped a cowbell to the end of my stick; so all the guys knew to get out of the way when they heard me coming. The coaches, the trainers, the players…everybody loved it."

And not only are Hartnell's wipeouts a source of humor, they're also a catalyst for raising money for good causes.

In early 2012, Hartnell founded the #Hartnell Down Foundation as a way to help charities that support hockey, children, and communities around the United States and Canada. It started from a Twitter following, keeping track of the number of times Hartnell would fall down during the NHL season. When Hartnell himself joined Twitter, he embraced the

---

104. Including two goals in Game 6 of the Finals.

catchphrase and began to sell merchandise with the proceeds going to Hartnell's favorite hockey-related charities.

Community oriented, Scott makes his home in the Old City neighborhood.

"I'm only a few blocks from the Liberty Bell, and I like to take a walk around," he says. "And it's kinda neat just to peek over and see it. Sometimes you take those kinds of things for granted. Last summer I ran across the Ben Franklin Bridge a couple of times just for a warm up, and it was really neat."

Scott is a big fan of the city. But what does he think about its notorious rooting base?

"Philly fans are intense. They're passionate," he says. "You'd rather have them on your side rather than on your back, yelling at you when you're on the other team. The GMs and Mr. [Ed] Snider have done a great job of having a tough team, of making it tough for opposing teams to come in here, because that's the model the Flyers had back in the 70s: 'If we can't beat ya on the scoreboard we're gonna beat the [stuff] out of you.' They're bar none probably the most intense and passionate of all the teams....If you win here, they'll love ya till your last breath."

CHAPTER 20

CHRIS PRONGER

It's the Indian summer of 2011. The East Coast has withstood not only Hurricane Irene but also an earthquake that registered 5.8 on the Richter scale. The Delaware Valley has been plagued by a record-setting, 28-plus inches of rain, and the boys are back in town, reporting to training camp and fired up for the new season.

And Chris Pronger, age 37, has just been named Flyers team captain.

But this is hardly his first stint as an NHL team leader. Pronger has worn the coveted "C" on his sweater for the St. Louis Blues (1997–2003), as well as for the Anaheim Mighty Ducks in 2007, helping lead the team to win the Cup that year.

"I think you have to be who you are and play the way you've always played, whether you have a letter on your jersey or not," Pronger says. "If you're a leader, lead. This is my third time being captain of a team. So I think I understand what the job entails and what needs to be done and what my role is. Whether you have a letter on your jersey or not doesn't matter. When I was in Edmonton, I never wore a letter, and it didn't make me less vocal or less of a player in the locker room."

But let's go back to when it all began.

————

The year is 1979.

Four teams from the disbanded World Hockey Association enter the NHL as expansion franchises: the Edmonton Oilers, Winnipeg Jets, Quebec Nordiques, and New England Whalers[105].

NHL President John Ziegler announces that helmets will be mandatory for all NHL players, allowing an exception for players who signed their pro contracts prior to June 1 of that year.

After starting the season with a 5–2 win against the New York Islanders and a 9–2 loss to the Atlanta Flames, the Flyers did not lose again for nearly three months, a span of 35 games. To this day this magnificent streak stands as the longest undefeated streak in North American professional sports history.

And Chris Pronger, then five years old, is learning to play hockey a year after learning to skate on his first pair of tube skates.

"There was an outdoor rink about a block from our house, and playing pond hockey was an everyday occurrence in our household," Pronger says. "We were out there pretty much every day after school and on weekends. If we weren't playing at the outdoor rink, we were over at the town rink…always

---

105.   Later renamed the Hartford Whalers at the insistence of the Boston Bruins.

playing hockey of some sort, even if it meant shoveling to clear off a patch to be able shoot pucks or have a little game in your driveway. We also had some pretty spirited road hockey games back in the day, too, which were always fun."

A couple of years later, Pronger began to play organized hockey while continuing to play outdoors with neighborhood kids and kids from school. "The age range varied. I remember being about seven, and the older kids were 10, 11, 12, so you had to learn pretty quick or you were left behind," he says. "It was good to get to play against older kids like that at an early age. It forced you to step up your game a little bit. We used to trade skates around. You got someone's hand-me-downs, and someone else got your hand-me-downs, and so on, and so on.

"Nowadays you watch these kids, and it's hockey 24/7/365. When I grew up when April came around, I was done [with hockey]. I was golfing, I was swimming, I was playing at the beach, outside riding my bike—you know, just being a kid. I was never even thinking about hockey."

Chris' hometown, Dryden, is a small city in southwestern Ontario where the closest town was Kenora, about an hour and a half away. "We never went to Toronto or Quebec or any of those big tournaments," he says. "The furthest we usually traveled was about six hours."

Although it's quite rural, Dryden is known by passers-by as the home of "Max the Moose"—Dryden's 18-foot high "mascot," a statue situated on the Trans-Canada Highway—as well as its annual Moosefest, a festival which boasts musical performances, children's activities, and a fishing tournament known as the Walleye Masters. But as loveable as Max is and as beautiful as moose can be, as Chris began to travel for hockey, he found that aside from being at a geographical disadvantage, there was also another impediment to traveling for hockey.

"When we were driving to tournaments and stuff, you had to watch out for moose," Pronger says. "You're laughing, but I'm dead serious. There were so many moose. You think your car gets messed up hitting a deer? Imagine the damage a moose can do. You hit one, and you're done. I remember moose running alongside of us as we drove along. You really had to be on the lookout, especially at night."

Even at an early age, Pronger knew on some level what separated the good players from the great ones: passion. He says, "As you look back on it, I mean, I'm from a small town in the middle of nowhere. So the commitment it was going to take [on my part]…whether it was me in my driveway shooting pucks on net or against the garage door for hours on end, having to shovel a couple feet of snow at the outdoor rink so we could have a chance to use it and skate on it…all these things teach you commitment and work ethic and dedication.…You can pull up probably 20 different adjectives, but it has to be a passion, because sometimes it takes a lot of work to get prepared to do what you want to do out there."

CHRIS PRONGER

The year is 1989.

Game 3 of the World Series is postponed due to the Loma Prieta earthquake—6.9 on the Richter scale—that strikes San Francisco moments before the game is set to begin. Phillies legend Mike Schmidt tearfully announces his retirement from baseball. And at Veterans Stadium, the visiting Pittsburgh Pirates score 10 runs in the top of the first inning, prompting Pirate broadcaster Jim Rooker to announce on air, "If we lose this game, I'll walk home." Two pairs of home runs hit by Von Hayes and Steve Jeltz trigger a comeback for the Phillies, who then take the lead on Darren Daulton's two-run single, to ultimately win the game 15–11. After the season, Rooker makes good on his promise and conducts a 300-plus-mile charity walk from Philadelphia to Pittsburgh.

And it is just occurring to Chris, now 15 years old, that he may have a shot at playing in the big leagues.

"Probably when I left home and started playing Junior B in Stratford [is when it first occurred to me]. You start comparing yourself to other players," Pronger says. "I hadn't yet had the opportunity to play against any elite-caliber players or the so-called 'top kids' in the Toronto area. So I got the chance to go down there and go to these different under-17, under-18 tournaments and started playing with these guys who were highly touted as top picks in the next NHL draft, and you start asking yourself, 'Well, is he really any better than me?' And I think at that point, you start seeing what people are saying about the players that you're playing against and you start matching yourself up against them and you realize that maybe you do have a chance.

"Good coaches see something in you, and they put in the time and effort to help you. I had a high school coach that took the time to work with me. Jack McMaster saw something in me and really worked with me to help develop my skills to get to the next level. You need coaches that are willing to sacrifice some of their own time to help you get better. That's where, as you go along, you get a greater appreciation for the whole volunteer side of youth sports. Especially those folks that were such a big part of your life growing up and such a big part of your career back then. And once you've been able to make it, they get to see you succeed like when Jack was able to come down to my Stanley Cup party in Anaheim. For the two of us to hold the Cup together…it was great."

But we're getting ahead of ourselves.

Pronger had two noteworthy seasons with the Peterborough Petes of the OHL, where he was named to the OHL First All-Star Team. He also won the CHL Plus/Minus Award; the CHL Best Defenseman Award; the Max Kaminsky Trophy, awarded to the Most Outstanding Defenseman of the OHL; and was a formidable defender for the Canadian Team that won the gold medal at the World Junior Championships. After Pronger earned those accolades, the Hartford Whalers selected him second overall in the 1993 NHL Draft.

His early NHL career included being named Whalers' Best Defender, earning a spot on the NHL's All-Rookie Team, and being named to Team Canada's roster for the 1998 Winter Olympics, where he was the team's youngest player.

But Pronger really came into his own during the 1999–2000 season. Plus-52 and with a career high of 62 points, he led the Blues to their best season ever and was awarded the Norris Trophy[106] as well as the Hart Trophy—the first defenseman to win it since Bobby Orr in 1972.

Pronger moved on to the Edmonton Oilers in 2005, where his solid contribution propelled the Oilers to the Stanley Cup Finals, before heading to Anaheim, where he helped the Ducks set new franchise records for wins (48) and points (110), ultimately winning the Cup in '07.

"When you played Philly, you always knew you were in for a tough game, whether it was going to be from the Flyers…or their fans," he says. "[The fans] are always vocal. They're always into it, and I think if I had played in the Eastern Conference and had gotten to come here and had some playoff series here or had been a part of one of those rivalries, that would've changed, I'm sure, my outlook on them and their outlook on me.

---

106. Given to the NHL defenseman who demonstrates throughout the season the greatest all-around ability at the position.

"The city has changed a lot since I first turned pro in 1993. It's always been a blue collar, blood-and-guts type of town, and while it still has those dynamics, the city itself has evolved. There's been a lot of development, a lot of cleanup projects. Just look at the athletic amenities: there's three top-notch sports complexes all in the same area, and now with Philly Live in its beginning phases…it's a pretty impressive setup for sports fans to come and enjoy their teams."

Pronger has made the playoffs with every team he has ever played for except for the Whalers and in every season except for his two with the Whalers. No team, that traded Pronger away, qualified for the playoffs the following year.

"I've been fortunate enough to play on some good teams and I hope to continue that streak, but not just make the play-offs, to get in there and do some damage. All you need is that opportunity," he says. "Once you're in, anything can happen. I think we've seen that in the past couple of years. You just never know."

Pronger's 19 years in the NHL has given him exceptional experience and priceless insight, and young aspiring athletes and their well-meaning parents would be wise to heed the advice the Flyers' team leader has to offer.

"The biggest thing is to enjoy yourself," he says. "The whole point of the game is to have fun. As a parent you want your kid to learn social skills, teamwork, camaraderie, supporting your teammate or your friend, being there for one another—all those things that are a part of a hockey team. All those things you learn from sports spill over into life and school…hard work, dedication—all those things that it takes to progress in sports and progress in life. But if you're telling your kid [you] have to do something, 'You *have to* do this, and you have to do that,' eventually they're going to get burned out and they're going to hate the sport because it's not *their* passion. It's their *parents'* passion. When I was four and I learned to skate, my parents asked me if I wanted to play hockey, and I said 'No,' and they said 'Okay.' So I just learned how to skate and that whole year I watched my brother play and I realized I wanted to play. So the next year, when they asked again, I said 'Yes.' So even now, I ask my kids if they want to play. My seven year old, for example, I asked him if he wants to play hockey this year and he said, 'No, I want to play soccer.' And I said, 'All right. Whatever, man. You're not going to hurt *my* feelings.' My older son plays, my middle son doesn't. He still likes to come out on the ice and screw around, but he's just not playing organized hockey right now. Will he in the future? I don't know. If he wants to, he can, but he's certainly not going to get any pressure from me."

CHAPTER 21

JAMES VAN RIEMSDYK

One of the greatest rivalries in the NFL is between the Philadelphia Eagles and the Dallas Cowboys, and it was probably best evidenced during the tempestuous Bounty Bowls of the late 1980s.

The year is 1989, and during the Cowboys' annual Thanksgiving Day game, the Eagles win 27–0, the only shutout Dallas has suffered during the annual game. The match is rough and hot-tempered, even by NFL standards. Among the many scuffles, Cowboys kicker (and former Eagle) Luis Zendejas suffers a concussion and was knocked out of the game after a particularly hard hit, prompting Dallas coach Jimmy Johnson to accuse Eagles coach Buddy Ryan of placing bounties on Zendejas and quarterback Troy Aikman. Just 17 days later, the teams would meet again at a snow-laden Veterans Stadium. Fueled by beer and Johnson's accusation, the infamously raucous Eagles fans throw seemingly anything they could get their hands on—from ice to batteries—at apparently anyone in sight. CBS broadcasters Verne Lindquist and Terry Bradshaw have to dodge snowballs in the broadcasters' booth. One referee is pelted and knocked to the ground. Jimmy Johnson has to be escorted from the field by Philadelphia police, and even Eagle

Jerome Brown becomes a target when he stands on the players' bench and pleads with the crowd to stop.

And it is also the year that James van Riemsdyk—or JVR as Flyer fans affectionately call him—is born, a New Jersey native who would grow up cheering for the New York Rangers, another notorious Philadelphia rival.

"I understand it's a pretty intense rivalry. And my dad, you know, he'd get pretty fired up, watching the games and stuff," he says. "But I think now that I'm on this side of it, I can appreciate some of the things that kind of drive you wild about [the Flyers] when you're on the other side of it. It's pretty cool now how that works. You don't expect it to work out this way, and now that I'm here, it's definitely been awesome.

"It's one of those things where you'd love to have them [Flyers fans] on your side, but if they're cheering against you, it's pretty brutal because they're ruthless out there. Even with us, they're not shy about letting us know when they're not happy with how we're playing. But it's a good thing. It keeps you honest. And it's definitely exciting to play in a place where people care that much. I would say that Flyers fans are the most passionate fans in the league, along with those Canadian cities like Montreal, Toronto."

But although JVR grew up a Rangers fan, he went to Devils games, too. "I was actually there in 2003 when the Devils beat the Ducks for the Cup," he remembers.

JVR credits his dad for getting him involved in hockey.

Before eventually settling in Jersey where he played hockey recreationally, Mr. van Riemsdyk, a devout fan, was born in Montreal and moved, "All over the map," James says. "He always had games on and hockey videos on when I was a kid."

And how has JVR's dad adjusted to shifting his team allegiance?

"He's come around," he smiles. "I think it's one of those things when you're rooting for a team, the opponents are portrayed in a different light…but when you kind of go behind enemy lines and get on the other side of things, I think you realize that it's just part of the game and how things work out sometimes.

"I would say my dad probably gets to make it to about 60-ish Flyers games a year. Almost all the home games, then the Devils, Islanders, Rangers…and he does a lot of business in Canada, too. So he always tries to work it so he can incorporate a business trip with coming to see me play, too."

But we're getting ahead of ourselves.

It probably comes as no surprise and perhaps is even expected that most Canadians learned to skate outdoors, especially in decades past. But it's a bit remarkable that James van Riemsdyk, who grew up in Middletown Township, New Jersey, and is just 23 years old, did, too.

"My first time skating was on a river in Connecticut at age one or two," he says. "We were visiting some family that lived up there outside Darian, and I remember having those double runners on—that you put on your shoes basically—and from there I played on natural ice at a rink in Old Bridge [New Jersey] that just had a roof and was only open in the winter."

James also recalls "jumping at any chance" he got to play outdoors when the winters were cold enough to allow the Jersey lakes and ponds to freeze. "It didn't happen every winter, but when it did we'd just try to get out there as much as we could," he says. "Whenever there was a chance, when the conditions would allow for it, we'd play outside. We loved it."

Another favorite spot to skate was the Navesink River, a major recreational venue that plays host to many water sports from boating and sailing and rowing to canoeing and kayaking, as well as crabbing, fishing, bird watching, and swimming. During particularly cold winters, the river freezes, adding ice skating and ice boating to its repertoire. The ice boats in particular could be an issue for hockey players, who often had to find creative ways to avoid them. JVR recalled another obstacle, "A funny thing was, if you'd miss a pass, and the puck would shoot past you, that puck is gone," he says.

———

JVR began playing organized hockey in 1993.

"I was four when I started playing some clinics and playing on some house leagues," he says. "Then I moved up to travel [Wall American Hockey]. The American Eagles were the first organized team I played on when I was a Mite, so about six or seven. I played three years for the Eagles, then moved onto Squirts [in Brick, New Jersey] through first-year Midgets.

"We also had an outdoor roller hockey rink called Normandy Park just a couple miles from my house, and we'd go there two-three times a week and just play for hours on end, just horsin' around. It was great."

Although it's understandable that a lot of the hockey greats from yesteryear never felt any pressure, JVR is a new breed of player—a young buck whose travel-team days are just a stone's throw behind him. So did he feel any pressure to play in an era when youth athletics have turned into an entirely different beast altogether?

"No. Not at all. I think my dad was really good about that sort of stuff," JVR says. "He obviously helped us when we needed help, but he never crossed that line of being one of those psycho parents that you hear all too much about these days. I think the key really is to just have fun with it. I mean if your goal is—when your kid is first trying a sport—if your goal is to have your kid become a professional athlete...well, I think that's pretty crazy because the odds of that happening aren't very good. But I mean if you just lead them in the direction and just let them have fun with it and let their passion grow for it, then I think you never know what can happen from there. But don't put the pressure on them to light the world on fire, when they're seven years old, or else they'll get burnt out."

And he should know. After all, JVR was always a standout. "Not everyone played hockey. So I guess some people looked up to me a little bit because I did play," he says. "And I guess I was pretty advanced for my age."

Yet he never got burnt out.

"I always loved it. I loved everything about it. I think the key for me was that I played for the same club for a long time, so I had a lot of great friends there," JVR says. "And while I could have moved up and played for different clubs, I played Tier 2 all growing up when I could have easily played Tier 1 for a lot of different places—but I think a big part of the reason why playing hockey was always so much fun for me was that I played with my friends, and we had different goals for our group. And we accomplished those goals together. We just had a great group of guys, and that's the key: having that bond with a good group of guys, and you're all on the same page....I probably still keep in touch with six or seven guys that I played with since I was eight years old. So it's really cool in that regard."

In pursuit of hockey, JVR transferred from Christian Brothers Academy after his sophomore year to move to Ann Arbor, Michigan to play for the U.S. National Development team, where he stayed with a billet family.

"After my first year in Ann Arbor when I was going into my senior year of high school, that's when I really thought it could eventually happen," he says. "I was rated pretty highly in the draft rankings and stuff. So it was then that I kind of realized that this might be something I could really pursue."

Selected second overall by the Flyers in the 2007 NHL Draft, JVR was just behind No. 1 pick and fellow American, Patrick Kane, marking the first time in NHL history that two Americans were drafted first and second overall in the same draft.

JVR was still in college at the time, attending the University of New Hampshire, a place he still has fond memories of, particularly when it came to playing pranks in the locker room.

"There's a couple of good ones that I've seen growing up. I think the water in the helmet is a good one. When, in their locker room stall, you just set a cup of water in their helmet so they can't see it, but when they pull it off to go on the ice they get drenched," he says. "I've seen some in college, where you take the knob off of someone's composite stick, and fill it up with water all the way to the top, and put the knob back on, and they go out there [on the ice], and they don't know what's going on, why their stick feels so weird. It makes it really heavy, and then obviously you can never use the stick ever again because it's ruined at that point."

In April 2009, the Flyers announced that van Riemsdyk would forgo his last two years of college eligibility to sign an entry-level NHL contract starting in the 2009–10 season; he then spent the remainder of the 2008–09 season playing for the Adirondack Phantoms on an amateur tryout contract, where he was initially expected to spend the year—or at best gain a place midway through the season—however, young James had another plan in mind.

During the annual rookie game against Washington, JVR had four goals and an assist, adding considerably to the 7–3 stampede against the Capitals, but that was only the beginning.

Catching the eyes of all watching, JVR was added to the Flyers starting 2009–10 roster alongside Claude Giroux, where he recorded his first NHL point in his inaugural game—an assist on a power play goal by Mike Richards in a 2–0 Flyers victory against the Carolina Hurricanes.

He returned to his Jersey roots for his next game, where he contributed two more assists against the Devils.

Then, after his quick return from a mild concussion during the Flyers' home opener, that forced him to miss two games, he scored his first goal on October 24, 2009 against Tomas Vokoun of the Florida Panthers.

The following month, however, is one every rookie likely dreams of. Not only did he record four goals and five assists, but three of those goals were game-winners, securing his well-earned honor as the NHL's Rookie of the Month for November.

And the magic of JVR has dazzled us ever since, perhaps most impressively during the 2010 Eastern Conference semifinals.

Inconsistent during the regular season, the seventh-seed Flyers found themselves on the wrong end of a 3–0 series against the sixth-seed Bruins. Philadelphia mounted a comeback, only to find itself losing to the Bruins 3–0 in Game 7 without a hometown crowd to bolster them.

But then came JVR.

With 2:50 left in the first period, he scored his first career playoff goal, and the game's momentum shifted to the Flyers so much that many observers believe that had it not been for JVR's goal, the Flyers would have been dead in the water.

The Flyers went on to win the game 4–3 before eventually making history, winning the series 4 games to 3.[107]

For van Riemsdyk's game-changing goal, he was named the Bud Light Impact Player of the Game.

Another fabulous career highlight came on February 15, 2011, in a game against Tampa Bay when JVR recorded the so-called "Gordie Howe Hat Trick"—a dream still glinting in the eyes of most veteran players—with a goal, an assist, and a fight in the Flyers' first victory over the Lightning in the season series.

But he was just getting started.

On March 26, 2011, in a game against the New York Islanders, JVR recorded his first career NHL hat trick in the Flyers' 4–1 victory. Two of the three were scored in even-strength play, while the third came on a power play. What JVR remembers the most, however, is how so many members of his family

---

107. Not since the New York Islanders came back from a 3–0 deficit against the Pittsburgh Penguins in 1975 had a team won four games in a row to win an NHL playoff series.

were there to see it, including his aunts and uncles and, of course, his parents.

In the opening round of the 2011 Playoffs, JVR was instrumental to the Flyers' 4–3 series win over the Sabres, tallying four goals, including the eventual game-winner in the seventh game to help the Flyers advance.

And in spite of the eventual sweep by the Bruins in the next round, JVR did not disappoint, adding three goals in four games in that series. What is most impressive, however, is that despite only playing in 11 games, he finished third in the entire postseason in total shots with 70[108] and led the postseason in shots per game.

Spectacular to the end, he finished the 2010–11 regular season with career highs in points (40), goals (21), and plus/minus rating (plus-15).

"The Stanley Cup run that we had my first year is what I'm most proud of thus far in my career," he says. "Obviously you play all year to have that team success at the end of the day, and if you're on good teams, chances are you're going to be playing in this game for a lot longer time. So you can draw on that experience."

The Flyers traded van Riemsdyk to the Toronto Maple Leafs for defenseman Luke Schenn during June of 2012. Luke is the older brother of Flyers forward Brayden Schen. So as the Flyers

---

108. James van Riemsdyk came in third behind only Daniel Sedin and Ryan Kesler of the Vancouver Canucks.

make their push to return the Stanley Cup to Philadelphia, they will have to it without their former local star.

Van Riemsdyk, on the other hand, will try to return the Cup to another storied franchise, the Maple Leafs, who last won the title in 1967. While pursuing that goal, he can use the lessons he learned while helping the Flyers through the playoffs.

"You know I felt pretty fortunate my first year to be on a team that made it that far and was that close," van Riemsdyk says. "It makes you that much more driven to get back there."

ACKNOWLEDGMENTS

First and foremost, I'd like to express my deepest gratitude to Mr. Snider for the opportunity to embark on this project and for all of the gracious support along the way. This book was a labor of love for me, and I'm grateful for your kindness, your encouragement, and for allowing me to contribute in some small way to the tremendous legacy you have created.

Secondly, this project would not have been possible without the participation of the Flyers I was fortunate enough to interview. I am thankful for the time you took to talk with me and for the openness in which you shared your stories. Speaking to each of you about your love of the game, your teammates, and the Flyers organization was a humbling and inspiring experience, one that I am so grateful for. Thank you all so much.

Another key element of this endeavor was the fabulous Steve "Coatesy" Coates. Thank you so much for always making time for me, even when you already have a hundred other balls up in the air. I truly appreciate your help, as well as your friendship. I couldn't have done it without you!

Very special thanks to Rich Israel, Wade Clarke, Tom Fletcher, and Ben Messier.

Also several sources—Joe Pelletier's Greatest Hockey Legends. com (www.greatesthockeylegends.com); the Official Site of the Philadelphia Flyers (www.Philadelphiaflyers.com); the Official Site of the Hockey Hall of Fame (www.hhof.com); and *In the Crease: Goaltenders Look at Life in the NHL* by Dick Irvin—were invaluable toward my research.

To my new friends at Triumph Books: Mitch Rogatz, Adam Motin, Andy Hansen, and Jeff Fedotin…thank you for everything you have done—and continue to do—to make this project a success.

I'd also like to thank Zack Hill, Ann Marie Nasuti, Shawn Tilger, Linda Held Mantai, Peg Murphy, and Meghan Winner for all of their wonderful support.

To my parents: thank you for everything. I love you very much.

And last but certainly not least…to the loves of my life, Sutton and Judd…just like the fine men in this book, I hope and pray all of your dreams will come true. Mommy loves you both beyond words. XOXO

Jakki Clarke with her father, Bobby, on November 15, 1984, the night the Flyers retired his jersey.

ABOUT THE AUTHOR

A former political operative who spent more than a decade on Capitol Hill and in the Northeast, the youngest daughter of Hall of Fame hockey legend Bobby Clarke seemed to have the drive to succeed in her blood from day one. And while she thrived in the competitive arena of partisan politics, she decided to make her graceful exit from that world to pursue her one true love: writing.

Born and raised in the Delaware Valley, she spent the bulk of her time competing in various sports and playing with the children of her dad's teammates, many of whom are still friends. Today she resides in Haddonfield, New Jersey, where she is currently working on her third novel, a harrowing political thriller set in Philadelphia.